Short Hops Acro...

Readers' comments

If you love aeroplanes and true-life gutsy flying adventures, you will love reading this book. Colin's gentle conversational and engaging style will have you turning page after page as if possessed. When I fly across the Atlantic it is with a crew of at least seventeen, plus several hundred passengers, the best support and back-up on the planet – and most essentially, four turbofan engines. Technically precise, often witty you'll laugh out loud in places, incredibly informative and filled with poignancy. Short Hops Across the Atlantic is a tribute, not only to Colin Cox, but also to everyone who has ever undertaken this amazing but very daunting challenge with one or maybe even two piston engines. With little or no support, a huge amount of personal discipline and professionalism, flying across some of the most inhospitable but spectacular topography in the world - and Colin kept on doing it! This book will have you riveted. Enjoy.

Captain Barry Eustance – Airbus A340-600   Major long haul airline.

This book should be in every pilot's bookcase & those interested in good true adventure stories, crossing the Atlantic Ocean and the Greenland Ice Cap is not for the unprepared.

Jeff Scott - American Flyer.

A light hearted book with a good sense of feeling

Hamilton (Canada) Heritage Museum.

A good read   - **Pilot magazine UK**.

A very enjoyable book with many memories.

Robin Mackay, Fairoaks Airport General Manager (retired).

Written with humour, plenty of photos & information in an easygoing style – look out for the 10,000-ton cloud!

Roger Nicklin PPL/IR pilot.

Front cover picture of a Piper Seneca – one of many I have flown, and a perfect light plane with which to enter the twin engine world.

Rear cover picture Goose Bay, Labrador ready off to Greenland.

Book details:

From the warmth of the Caribbean, up the east coast of America, north through Canada, across to Greenland and the infamous ice cap, then to Iceland, and finally down to the UK .

Printed by:
Print Domain

Graphic designer:
g.pensri@pensri.co.uk
www.pensri.co.uk

First edition autumn 2005
Second edition winter 2009

ISBN number: ISBN 978-0-9550745-1-6

Published by Colin Cox

Author Colin Cox
All copyrights belong to the author

All rights reserved

No part of this publication may be reproduced, stored in a retrieval system, or transmitted, in any form or by any means, without the express permission in writing of the publisher.

Website
www.shorthopsacrosstheatlantic.com
colin@shorthopsacrosstheatlantic.com

CONTENTS - Short Hops Across the Atlantic

- 4   Index
- 5   Dedication
- 6   Author's notes
- 8   The pilot
- 9   The beginning
- 11   Her Majesty Is Not Amused
- 20   Nudist Invasion alert
- 22   First Hop
- 39   Second *(BIG)* Hop by British Airways
- 45   A Hop around Florida
- 57   Alligator on the runway
- 67   A Short Hop - The Wrong Way
- 71   Bahamas Hop
- 94   An Extremely Short Hop
- 111 A Goodbye to Sunny Florida Hop
- 129 Boston Closed
- 131 The 10,000-ton cloud
- 138 The highest tide in the world
- 145 The *(French)* Canadian Hop
- 149 A Further North Hop
- 157 Onward North through Newfoundland and Labrador Hop
- 174 A Potentially Wet Hop to Greenland
- 185 A Welcome To Greenland Hop
- 206 A *(Delayed)* Local Test Flight Hop
- 218 Weather to go or whether not to, Greenland to Iceland Hop
- 233 A Hop towards the Haggis
- 240 South across the Border Hop
- 242 The end of a Hop
- 247 General Information, Pilot licence etc.
- 248 Acknowledgements

THIS BOOK IS DEDICATED TO THE TRUE PIONEERS OF YESTERYEAR, ESPECIALLY THE AVIATOR WHO WENT FORWARD INTO THE UNKNOWN WITHOUT THE SOPHISTICATION AND KNOWLEDGE OF TODAY.

`Bring forth your dream from the depths of your mind, lest it be forgotten in the rush of day, for tomorrow will come even if we sleep, but the dream may slip away`.

Colin Cox January 2004

To my wife Beate, and my children Liam and Ella, for being a patient and loving family.

In memory of my dear friend Denis who found and lived his dream.

Also in memory of Gillian who always wanted me to write this book.

My grateful thanks to Sarah, Denis's wife, who did the proof reading.

Author's Notes:

Flying in today's modern world is a very straightforward affair and an extremely safe way of getting around our beautiful world. It is well worth looking back to yesteryear and remembering how our pioneering brethren risked their lives in the pursuit of advancement. Little planes can still be a dangerous mode of transport, given their fragility in turbulent weather, along with the lack of duplication of essential systems that large planes have in abundance. We need air to breathe and to live, but it is a medium ever unforgiving to those who venture into the blue yonder without due care; a scrooge waiting in a corner to take all and to give nothing in return!

Today, we are more akin to adventurers than pioneers, satisfying our own desire for exploration – yesterday the pioneers were satisfying the world's desire for progress.

In this ever-changing world, it is now possible to go virtually anywhere - from the fringes of outer space to the depths of the oceans and the extremes of the Poles. Let us think for a moment and remember the way of life that has passed - those thousands of men and women pioneers - adventurers who have gone before us. They would not understand our world of today, but we need to look back to their world, so we can face the future with equanimity.

This photo clearly shows the utter desolate blackness of space, and just how beautiful our planet is illuminated by the sun, compared with our nearby planets devoid from the life we know.

Half a world! Night time from the blizzards and icy wastes of west Iceland and down through the sun drenched tropical beaches of western Africa where a new dawn heralds a new day and new hope for so many. Ever onwards, night time dissecting the world somewhere near Australia before continuing around the other side. Half a world slumbering, while the rest of the world is getting up. So the cycle of life continues day in, day out. At night, flying westwards you can follow the day, and catch up the time that has passed. Flying eastwards the sun is your friend, ever waiting for you on the horizon - as we were to find out on our hop across the icy wastelands of the snow-capped mountains of Greenland, and the Atlantic Ocean.

The pilot
(Written by Ella, daughter of the author, at the age of 12)

There he was, walking down as if he has a mission and won't stop until it is complete. He glides swiftly along as if he's walking on air down the corridors of the airport. He is oblivious to the surroundings and continues to pass families and friends gathering to say their goodbyes. He has no time for waiting and weaves in and out through the queue, flashing his ID card to Security. He passes on. He steps onto the plane as the airline staff welcome him aboard. He waits. Waits for his passengers to arrive on the plane. He sits in his seat - waiting. His golden hair peeking out from under his captain's hat glistens in the sunbeams. His broad shoulders and powerful arms stretch out wide. Getting ready for a long journey ahead and for him to take his passengers there. That is his mission. He takes off his jacket and hangs it behind the door, showing the epaulettes on his shoulder pads. Stripes are an honour the more you had, the more important you are. One stripe for a pilot in training, two stripes for a flight engineer, three stripes for a co-pilot and four for captain. The airline staff gave the safety talk and rules and the captain took the plane off and away. He concentrates deeply and focuses on the destination even though it was thousands of miles away. He begins to lay back and pushes the switch to autopilot. He is relaxed. It seems like this is the only place that he can be relaxed. Up in the air as quiet as can be. You can see him sitting back and waiting until the opportune moment to move out of his seat. It's like he has a schedule inside his head and he would stick to it .There he was. Thinking of thoughts and dreams that are a complete mystery. No one can figure him out, or what his hopes are…his dreams…his fears.

The Beginning

*"Cessna 336 registration **G**olf **P**apa **I**ndia **X**-ray **S**ierra, you are cleared to enter Heathrow Control zone and to continue to central London. Identify yourself under special security code clearance".* I punched in the all-important ID on our transponder; not wishing to be interrogated by a nervous pilot in a military plane with his finger ready on the `fire` button. I turned to Denis sitting in the co-pilot's seat and said how things have changed from the pre-terrorists days. He murmured in agreement as I made a gentle turn to position the aircraft 1,500 feet over the financial capital of the world, preparing for a `photographic shoot` of London`s central Banks.

Pilots spend a lot of time pushing buttons on the radios and various other instruments, dialling in frequencies and messing about with other electronic gadgets in the cockpit. I remembered that in my mid-teens in the late 1950`s and early 1960`s, being intrigued by dials and knobs I used to frequent jumble sales in a hunt for old-fashioned valve radios. I used my hard-earned pocket money, obtained by riding a rickety old bike to deliver newspapers in all types of weather, including thunderstorms, ice and snow. I managed to avoid those motorists who were up and about at that unearthly hour, but the odd guard dog hiding in the undergrowth would certainly spice up the delivery round as he tried to give you a nip on the leg! However the bonus was being able to read various children's comics during the daily early morning excursions. Reading all the exciting adventures of my comic book heroes probably planted the seeds of exploration in my mind, and learning not to get lost in the myriad of roads in the housing estates set my mind with a sense of direction.

Occasionally, people would see this strange youth staggering along the road carrying some ancient radio housing a mass of wires, resistors, capacitors, valves and of course knobs. Much to my parents' consternation, I would happily spend a weekend blowing the odd fuse and receiving more than my fair share of electric shocks in a sometimes successful attempt to get a radio operational. A fairly often occurrence was the neighbours knocking on the door thinking the house was on fire or under attack after seeing smoke billowing out of the window and my screaming at yet another painful electric shock.

Take a look into the cockpit of any modern airliner to see that knobs and buttons have been replaced with digital flow meters, finger touch controls, large LCD screens, voice assisted control functions - all in a blazing glory of colours; no black & white today. Somehow not quite the same as it used to be! Nevertheless, I am sure that the pilots still have fun – with perhaps a little wishful thinking of the good old days when there were more buttons to be pressed. In any case, there is still the odd lever needing a shove in the right direction.

Her Majesty Is Not Amused

Denis had an aerial photo job to do above the new Charing Cross Station. This made a change from doing aerial road mapping work. He was sitting in the back of the twin engine Cessna 336 in his usual place with pieces of camera gear, sticking plaster holding lengths of cable together, and films everywhere; no digital cameras in those days. A flask of coffee *(cold)*, a scattering of sandwich wrappers, and the odd stale crust complete the scene. Denis's idea of a working lunch was him huddled in the back munching away like a little squirrel, and me holding a sandwich in one hand, flying with the other and spitting out breadcrumbs like a machine gun when talking to Air Traffic Control. It was more often than not a working lunch, as we always seemed to be in the middle of a job when that all-important mealtime arrived.

The redeeming feature was that occasionally, if a job had been really successful, it had been known for Denis, in a fit of madness, to throw all caution to the wind and gesticulate with his hands the shape of a wine glass, indicate he was hungry by rubbing his tummy, and then yell, *"Head due south to Dinard"*! Although in the past flight plans for crossing borders were normally made on the ground, they can be accepted by the ATC in the air if I/we can think of a good reason why we cannot land and do things in the normal way. However, we were in an ever-changing era and this part of flying was getting more pilot friendly, and I can sound mighty convincing on the radio when there is French food at the end of the flight! Dinard being south of the channel islands was an even better incentive, as on the way back, I would drop into Alderney *(still one of my favourite destinations)*, and fill up the tanks with duty free fuel. A brief stopover there, then some low flying back over the English Channel gazing at the ships ploughing through the waves below. Eventually reaching the white cliffs of The Needles at the entrance to the Solent and reluctantly heading back to Fairoaks.

Both Denis and I had a passion for French wine and French food, so it was a special treat to go charging off to the other side of the English

12

Channel to eat. He was a generous person with great character and it was easy to spend a very pleasurable time chatting over lunch whilst the midday passed into late afternoon, forgetting that we should be photographing something or someone back in England! Appreciating the lovely food, I was denied the pleasure of wine, *(pilot rules on drink and flying are the same if not more severe than vehicle drink and driving),* and stuck to boring mineral water whilst recovering from the headache which always plagued me after being ensconced in the deafening noise of the cockpit.

The Cessna 336 is one of the noisiest small six- seat twin-engine planes ever built. It is certainly not a plane for long hops – a bit like an old Land Rover – which would get you there ok but you would be denied the pleasure of the quiet and comfortable interior of a saloon car. However, the 336 was perfect for photographic work especially over London; with three seats removed there was plenty of room for Denis to roll around along with all his equipment. Maybe not `rolling` around but Denis was certainly usually creeping around on all fours dealing with the cameras, and also watching out for the right hand side door which had a habit of opening when in flight. I was ever ready to bank sharply to the left to keep him in the plane should this happen! I eventually `twigged` the reason why I only ever got paid after the flight – Denis's insurance, just in case I happened to forget to bank at the vital moment. Needless to say parachutes were not an option, besides which, we were too low and the chute would have opened just as we would have been starting the breaststroke across the Serpentine in Hyde Park.

Although we both had headphones, Denis would often shout various headings to me in his excitement to obtain the best position to take the photos. He seemed to forget that I could hear him through the intercom though not very clearly. This was not the modern quiet cockpit of some luxury business jet where the pilots use small secretarial type headpieces. The items we were using would probably attract the interest of the London Science Museum such was the antiquity and rarity of our ancient headgear. In fact, I swear the weight of these archaic lumps extended my ear lobes a little each year. Even the push-to-talk button on the control yoke was more in keeping with a sharp nail since the little rubber cap disappeared somewhere between Florida and London. Wincing every time the button was pressed, I used to wrap a piece of camera tape around my thumb for protection. With Denis waving in the back and me trying to talk to Control, we must have made an amusing pair.

Certainly there was no shortage of fresh air in this plane - whilst taking photographs both windows were open, along with a large round hole in the floor for the vertical camera. The hole was not used to tip out our accumulated rubbish - we were very `green` in more ways than one, and all our litter was disposed of in a careful way – usually Denis throwing something at me to ensure that I was still awake!

The particular job that day was near home so the flight was a quick affair, taking some 15 minutes from Fairoaks airport by Woking to Charing Cross Station. Vastly quicker than driving, besides which, it is fun going up the A3 towards London at 140 miles an hour, albeit 1,500 feet above the road, especially when passing the odd police car. The driver probably wondered what on earth the awful din was thundering overhead. The noise alone would have made him jump through the roof, let alone seeing some beaten up old relic flying past, and I am talking about the plane not the pilot!

Forty minutes later with another job over, and bearing in mind our low altitude and speed, I made a gentle turn to port towards our airfield, paying special attention to the plane remaining straight and level in the turn. The 336 likes the ground and has a habit of nose-diving just when you are not expecting it. This means putting both feet on the instrument panel, pushing the power levers fully forward, and pulling back the control column between your legs with both hands. Shouting the battle cry of the American Indians, `Geronimo` helps! Denis meanwhile in the back not strapped in his seat would have completed three loops, one backward flip, and qualified to enter the Olympics.

I was expecting at this juncture of the flight that he would suddenly decide that the weather was perfect in Dundee for a road bypass job. This had been outstanding for a `wee` while and was urgently needed by the town planning authorities. Denis would merely yell to me, "*Change of plan Colin – head north for Scotland*". There was a small radio in the back of the plane secreted under the debris, which gave the forecasts of every airport in the country. When I was not looking, he would plug in his headset and listen for the latest observations – hence sudden changes of plan.

I could always tell that something was up when he went quiet and his head had disappeared under a pile of charts. The navigational chaos it caused me seem to pass him by. I would have to scrabble around for a map/chart and do some quick calculations. I had to ensure that we remained clear of controlled airspace, various airports en route and most importantly – other aircraft. The various sector traffic controllers knew us well enough by now after some 20 years of operation, and they would usually give a heading to keep me out of mischief until I had worked out a route to our destination. Meanwhile Denis would be engrossed in planning the photographic detail; bearing in mind that we had a flight of just over 2 hours, he had plenty of time on his hands! Strictly unofficial, occasionally we had the odd request from a Controller to fly over their airport and take a photo for them to put up on the canteen wall. Denis ever obliging would comply, as for sure we would be landing there sometime, and it could mean a free cup of tea and who knows – a biscuit as well.

The Cessna 336 lacked some operational extras; in fact, I would go as far as to say it lacked any extras! I also had to work without the luxury of an autopilot, which made flying quite tiring, especially as it was fitted with manual trim controls that needed constant attention. Fortunately, it was not one of those `heavy` flying days with last minute instructions to fly north. This was just as well as a few minutes later on the radio I heard, *"Golf – Papa India X-ray Sierra could you call the Heathrow Director after landing".* Oh dear what have I done now? Clearance from Fairoaks ATC was straight in on runway 24 (*an abbreviation for 240 degrees on the compass – near enough due west).* Complying with the Noise Abatement rule for this type of plane effectively means pulling back the power almost to zero and gliding like an air borne brick past one of the most legendary historic racing car tracks, Brooklands. It was previously a well-known airport, and now a museum of motor & aviation, with several large planes on the ground and no obvious reason as to how they got there. They looked out of place for the runway had all but disappeared into a concrete jungle of industrial buildings.

Onwards towards Fairoaks, passing over the M25, then over the lonely oak tree just by the threshold of the runway we landed back at base. One day, I am sure, someone will take out the tree or more than likely the tree will take out a plane.

As we rolled down the taxiway at a sedate speed of 10 mph, a spectator stood, fingers in ears, looking perplexed. The din created by the Cessna 336 obviously confused him probably thought the sound was that of some big jet not the modest 336, which hove into view! We continued on, and thundered noisily past the little café to the parking area. I stopped the engines, and made a mental note to get the oil leak fixed that I had noticed dripped onto the clean tarmac outside the hangar. I then breathed a sigh of relief as the deafening noise faded away, and dutifully called the Heathrow Director.

It appears that the Queen was having a garden party and my turn from our survey happened to take us directly over Buckingham Palace. The very fact that the turn started somewhere above Kingsway, normally would have been executed well before the Mall. Alas, it was not possible in this plane, and due to the slow speed and altitude the turn had to be gentle, and unfortunately ended just above Her Majesty. The 336 making such a racket had upset the Royal Household and no doubt a few others down beneath our wings. Had I made a right turn it would have taken us away from the Palace and towards the East End of London, but Docklands

Airport was in that direction, therefore it made sense to turn westward.

With due apologies and quietly thinking that a garden party might be better held in Balmoral, I said to Denis afterwards that maybe Cessna ought to design a quiet exhaust system similar to cars. It should be mentioned that in actual fact this was the second time we had received a complaint from Buckingham Palace. I was starting to feel a little guilty, and vowed that next time we came near the Palace I would pull back the power and glide past Her Majesty; not that the 336 was much of a glider, more like a flying van.

The airspace above our Capital gets pretty busy, and there is only a small vertical corridor between 1,000 and 2,500 feet that non-airline planes can fly between. Scheduled planes are coming into London Heathrow a few thousand feet above our heads; with more schedules coming into London City airport. Therefore, in our undersized segment, we have the police helicopter and security patrols buzzing around, plus Air Ambulances, and helicopters to Battersea Heliport. Then for good measure, Capital Radio's own Piper Seneca flies around giving out traffic reports. We may get stuck in traffic on Mother Earth, but in the air, it can also get very crowded.

The Air Traffic Control men and women do a fantastic job keeping us all in order and acting a little like a mother hen looking after her brood. I would imagine that on some days their radar screens would be so cluttered with aircraft that the images would look like a star wars invasion. Though today, with the expansion of Heathrow and the other major airports, the approach, landing and take-off phases are computer controlled; such is the complexity of the overcrowding of our skies over London.

Nudist invasion alert.

Now that made you sit up! It was not our fault, honestly; we were in the single engine Cessna 182 taking a series of photos of a dry flood plain not that far from our base. Denis had taken images of the same site during the winter, and now in the height of summer, the Local Authority wanted another set of shots in connection with a planning application from a well-known builder. No doubt the firm wanted to attract house buyers interested in fishing from their bedroom window, should the flood plain flood again!

A call came on the radio that a complaint had been made to the airport about us. Now being very good folk this was quite unusual, apart from the two incidents with Her Majesty. It appears that we had been flying over a very small private nudist colony during the circular orbits I was making over this particular area. The radio transcript went something like this.

20

(Control) "G-xxxx we have received a complaint from a private individual of you flying over their location several times, can you explain yourself"? (Me) "Yes Control, we are making six orbits around this area for our survey then we will be finished – is there a problem". (Control) "Err yes, um, you are flying over a private nudist colony and they think that you are taking photos of them". Denis's ears immediately pricked up, and he changed the lens on his camera in record time to a telephoto lens. *(Me - looking out and trying to fly the plane at the same time) "Err, um, Control this is G-xxxx can you give me the approximate location from your radar trace"? "Err, um, yes, G-xxxx can you avoid flying any further in the direction you are heading by turning left or right". (Me) "Say again Control",* by which time we had over flown the address *(undress)* one more time with Denis clicking away testing the camera for purely scientific and biological reasons.

I kid you not – that really did happen; what became of the photos I do not know. Though the Council did ask if they could have an enlarged version of the surrounding area – purely, you understand, for planning purposes!

First Hop

As with all stories there has to be a start and at the end, an end! It was Joe a musician friend of mine who introduced me to flying. One pleasant summer's day in 1982, Joe having a PPL *(private pilot's licence)*, hired a plane from Denham, a small airport near London, and we were to fly down to Cornwall. His parents had a farm, which included part of an old world war two airfield near Padstow, complete with prisoner of war buildings, various other derelict bits and an old control tower.

Whilst waiting for Joe to get the plane ready I looked around the airport. There was the usual assortment of planes on the grass, high wing, low wing, single engine and the odd twin. I also noticed several helicopters – they are noisier than most light aircraft including the Cessna 336, but the 336 is banned from some airports because it is so loud. That is a bit unfair, as helicopters never had that restriction.

Denham Airport had a golf club at one end of the runway and there was a sort of love hate relationship between the flyers and the golfers. Probably more hate than love where the golfers were concerned, as presumably the wind generated from the propellers would play havoc with the golf ball when transcending from ground to air and ground again!

You could hear the golfers cry out from their bunkers – *"mind your balls"* as another plane commenced its take off run.

Some years ago a Bristol Blenheim 2nd World War plane crash-landed onto the golf course. The twin-engine bomber had been beautifully restored taking thousands of hours to rebuild, but it met disaster when carrying out a low flypast over Denham runway. The pilot, more used to flying very large passenger jets, reduced power to carry out the low-level flight, and then increased the power immediately to maximum by pushing the throttle levers fully open. You can do that with a jet engine that needs at least 10/15 seconds to spool up and to reach max power – bearing in mind the heavy weight and inertia of the plane – or indeed with a modern fuel injected engine. But you cannot with a 60-year-old engine plane using old carburettors. The difference between power *(jet)* and throttle *(carburettor)* was that the engines simply stalled and the result was a very expensive plough. Fortunately, nobody was badly hurt, only in pride, but it did upset a great many enthusiasts who had spent so much voluntary time building the plane.

Various flying clubs had little buildings arranged around the perimeter, mainly for drinking tea. They resembled rustic garden sheds, with the odd flower vainly trying to survive the onslaught of the weeds, and the numerous cold cups of coffee and tea poured over them. Complete with dirty smudged windows for peering out of when the weather was a touch inclement, they would not have looked out of place in a wartime movie.

Hidden away in the corner of the airfield you would find the maintenance hangar. Here the aircraft engineers would shudder every time they heard an engine over boosted, and cry when they saw a plane bouncing along the runway instead of a smooth silky landing commonly known as a `greaser`. These were the experts who would lovingly repair, mend, clean and generally take care of the flying machines for the aviator. Like so many other locations, this is one of many places where the budding airline pilot starts the long uphill struggle to climb the tree of aviation to the airlines. Mind you, looking at the organised chaos at the big airports I prefer the relative peace of the small airstrips.

Lining up on Denham runway with all the pre-take off checks done, Joe, being a careful pilot, put his feet firmly on the brakes of the little 4-seat plane and opened the power to maximum before releasing the brakes. However, the plane did not seem to notice this applied increase of power. One of many things small planes are deficient in is the lack of acceleration, so applying full power before moving is a prudent move. Eventually we crept along the runway, and staggered into the air just before the end, keeping clear of the golfers and their balls!

We climbed westward in what can only be described as perfect flight conditions, with a cloudless blue sky.

Once clear of the messy suburbs and outlying towns we headed slightly south of west into open country. Many of the old airfields are now used to park the masses of cars manufactured and not sold; or they had been turned into housing estates. Over flying the old disused aerodromes, you could occasionally still see the outline embedded in the ground of the hangers and control tower.

Sometimes I wonder what would have happened if there had not been two world wars. Certainly, many people would have survived – but what of flying? The majority of airfields, airports, aerodromes, airstrips, call them what you will, would not have been around had we been at peace with everyone. Progress always seem to come at the expense of people. Virtually everywhere that had sufficient place for a runway - be it concrete, tarmac or grassy field - was used for that purpose during the last war.

It may be surprising to know that during the last two world wars Heathrow Airport was just a large grass field with a few huts. Croydon in Surrey was the first major `International` airport of its time. Starting in the early 1920`s the newly created fledgling airlines of the world, because of the lack of navigation beacons, used to follow roads, railway lines, rivers and other prominent landmarks in order to arrive at their destination.

When the weather was inclement, the initial accident rate was extremely high. Fortunately, passenger planes were very small and not too many people came to grief. Improvements to navigation came quickly on the scene to advance the safety record.

Joe checking the fuel contents with me waiting to go.

As we flew over Greenham Common by the town of Newbury in Berkshire, I remembered that only a few years before this airport was used as the first line of defence by the Americans against the enemy *(whoever they were),* and was bristling with nuclear missiles and underground silos. The fact that we, the UK, would have been annihilated in the process of protecting the USA all those thousands of miles away seems to have escaped the notice of our government, ever pleased to support our allies on the other side of the Atlantic Ocean. Probably 99% of

Americans never knew that their most advanced Eastern Strategic Missile Control Centre was by a racecourse near to a pretty rural English hamlet. There were countless anti-war, anti-nuclear protests; scores of people camped outside the perimeter fence by the main entrance for a non-stop 24-hour vigil that went on for years. Happily, it is now a large industrial estate and there is little left to indicate its former role.

Leaving Newbury and its buried silos behind us, we sat back and relaxed; the engine pulling us forward, and the wings lifting us ever higher through the air. Most light un-pressurised aircraft have to stay in the lower altitudes - which just happens to be where most of the bad weather hangs out. A few miles higher the big jets fly in relative comfort.

Navigation to the basic pilot is effectively map reading. You plot a course with the route marked clearly on the appropriate aeronautical chart, and keep a list of your pencilled notes giving the times when you should change direction. This would normally coincide with a prominent land feature to confirm the calculations – such as a major road junction, a river or a train station, etc. Our route was particularly simple, with Wales and the Bristol Channel on the right wing tip, and Somerset and Devon on the left. Flying at a lowly 1,600 feet, the fields lay below us as a large patchwork quilt of various colours. It was a beautiful sight until we approached the muddy Severn estuary swirling under the huge suspension bridge. You could see the currents of water in the tide rushing past sandbanks, which were more like very large lumps of glutinous mud. Certainly not a place for a forced landing – if you did not sink in the sludge, the fast currents of the waters would remove the plane in record time; either way would be very unpleasant.

The well-publicised Severn Bore at the top of the Bristol Channel is reputedly the second highest tide in the world; the difference between the lowest and highest tide in any one day can be more than 14.5 metres *(45 feet)*. Co-incidentally, the Bay of Fundy between New Brunswick, and Nova Scotia, some 3,000 miles west, has the highest tide in the world. It is on a similar latitude to the Bristol Channel and I have flown over it on return trips from America; but more on that later. As we flew over the Severn bore the whole mass of water seemed alive, a spectacular show by nature illustrating her power unleashed. Continuing westward towards our destination, you could see the motorway snaking its way through the Welsh countryside towards Newport, Cardiff and beyond. I saw several cars meandering on the bridge, and it was not because of the wind, just some drivers trying to look at the sights instead of concentrating on driving. They were perhaps unaware of the peril should they by chance meander too far, and disappear over the edge into oblivion in the turbid waters below.

The smaller roads lay in dells intermixed with the countryside. Trees formed a green canopy over small lanes, making them barely visible from the air. The odd car would suddenly appear out of a mass of green, only to be swallowed up again a few bends later; and railway lines rolled across the landscape. We even saw several crop circles with patterns that defy belief. Interestingly enough, I have found that crop circles always seem to be around military zones. Salisbury Plain with its connections to Stonehenge, pagan rituals and beliefs, seems to have more than its fair share of these mysterious runes. There has to be an answer somewhere, and no doubt the argument as to how these intricate patterns were made will go on indefinitely. One very inescapable and rather sad fact is the absence of any forest, let alone any really large wooded area. In fact, you have to look hard to find any large woodland in England apart from Robin Hood's Sherwood Forest in Nottinghamshire. This was quite noticeable later on when doing aerial work throughout the UK; I saw how much the land had been decimated to the detriment of the trees. Even on the flight with Joe, it was conspicuous that some of the fields had been enlarged by the removal of the all-important hedgerows. I think that sometimes we maybe try to copy the United States a little too closely. After all, they have a massive country and can afford to make their crop fields the size of one of our counties, but it does look rather odd in little old Britain. However, when reading John Steinbeck's classic `Grapes of Wrath`, I realised that the Americans had their fair share of soil deprivation and problems, albeit a long time ago, and due in part to the removal of hedgerows.

Clearing the Bristol Channel and Cardiff Control by flying in the middle of the waterway like some airborne ship, we continued towards Cornwall. It was truly a postcard scene, as we viewed the cliffs, hills, and small towns in the valleys. Trains are always fascinating to watch from the air as they rush along the track carrying people to their destinations. I would imagine in the old days it would have been even more thrilling with the steam engines puffing out their smoke into the skies; but let us remember the firemen who had to stoke the blazing furnace to propel the hissing steaming locomotives along the rails. Eventually Joe's airfield came into view, and we switched from discussing the size of the fields to noting the size and length of Joe's runway, which looked a little short! As we came into land, I could never have imagined I would be flying a similar plane from Miami, Florida a few years later.

Well, that was the first hop, literally. At the beginning of the strip, there was a high voltage electric pylon about 30 feet in the air, which some local electricity supplier had inconveniently put across the start of the runway. This meant that after a normal approach to landing one would pull the stick back at the last moment, encouraging the elevators to lift the plane above cables that would fry anyone foolish enough to touch them. We then dropped down quickly, ensuring that there was enough runway left before hitting the temporary fence at the other end - which kept the sheep out! I might add that the airstrip was private and only a few people were allowed to use the worn out 60-year-old airfield.

Safely on the ground, and with a group of sheep munching grass and cautiously watching us, we got out of the little single engine Grumman Cheetah and headed for Joe's Studio. This was the latter part of the heyday for groups such as the Moody Blues, Phil Collins, Dire Straits, Wizard, ELO, Pink Floyd, Supertramp and Cliff Richard, to name but a few. Joe was a leading guitarist with many groups and I got to know a couple of these incredible musicians and some of the mischief they got up to during their tours. Joe increased his fame when he played in Jeff Wayne's War of the Worlds double LP along with Richard Burton, Julie Covington, David Essex, Justin Hayward and others.

War of the Worlds was a frightening success in America, not so much the music but the much earlier radio broadcast. On October 30th, 1938, the United States experienced mass hysteria, most pronounced on the East coast in New York and New Jersey, in response to a radio broadcast put out by Orson Welles and his Mercury Theatre `On The Air`. This hysteria was no doubt compounded by the threat of the impending war in Europe. Remember that television was only just being developed. The radio was most people's contact with the outside world, and they were a little naive - listeners used to believe what they heard.

Covering the last one hundred years there have been several full length `War Of The Worlds` feature films. Unaccountably, some of the inhabitants of our planet seem to believe that there was a threat from the red planet Mars. Even today, when listening to the music, I get goose pimples down my spine. The following is an extract from a news article that followed the early broadcast.

The public reaction has prompted decades of research into mass hysteria, been used as a model by the military around the world to design information warfare against enemy troops and civilian populace, and used as the most compelling reason to protect the public from the knowledge of the presence of aliens on Earth.

A certain General Wilson had been conducting an alien white paper. It took him a little while, but he managed to pluck a file out of the morass of red tape over at the Pentagon, and this file reveals the truth of the Orson Welles `War of the Worlds` radio broadcast in 1938. The truth is, there actually was an alien invasion in a place named Grover's Mill. From our analysis of eyewitness reports conducted on the 50th Anniversary of Orson Welles' broadcast of `War of* *the Worlds`, it appears that in 1938 it was just a scouting mission, a group ahead of the main alien invasion to evaluate Earth's technological level and what to expect on arrival. The aliens were defeated, not by bacteria, but by the Grover's Mill Militia with the weapons they had on hand. It appears they (the aliens) did not have their `magnetic blister` shields to protect their ships.

Research: Orson Welles and H G Wells

It seems that the media will do anything for a good story. Especially when you think that the story from the films and music of The War of the Worlds was set in Horsell Common – a few miles south of London. I wonder what H G Wells would have made of it all? He wrote many brilliant futuristic books including `*War of the Worlds*` in 1898?

Joe, having received a gold disk for his efforts, was back to making more *(very loud)* music in the peace of the Cornish countryside in his converted studio. The old WW2 base was on top of a hill, only a couple of miles from the cliffs and the sea. I can imagine that with a north-westerly storm blowing, on a dark winter's night, it would be quite an intimidating place to be staying. However, whilst I was there, the weather was calm and glorious. I could even hear the birds singing in the hedgerows; which shows the sound absorbing qualities of the old concrete building where Joe was playing his latest piece at full volume. Whilst he was busy with his songs, I spent a pleasant few days walking around the ruins of the old wartime remains and imagining what it would have been like during the Battle of Britain. Certainly the Spitfires and Hurricanes would have made a lot of noise as they took off in search of the Hun. No doubt, *(jokingly)* had the aforementioned electricity pylon been in the way then, the pilots probably would have used it as target practice.

A normal single seat Spitfire, trust me to forget a camera when seeing the famous 2-seat trainer in the hangar. (File photo).

It was therefore with some surprise that walking into an old hangar, I saw in front of me, in all its glory, a Spitfire, not just a Spitfire, but one of the very rare 2-seat trainer types. It was being painfully and expensively restored for its owners. To see the plane half rebuilt with an engine the size of a small car was awe inspiring to say the least. With time to spare I did some research into the plane that along with the Hurricane saved Great Britain in its hour of need. The Spitfire was created and designed by Reginald Joseph Mitchell, the British aircraft designer, and it was one of the best-known fighters in WW II. After secondary schooling Mitchell was an apprentice at a locomotive works and attended night classes at a local technical college in Southampton. In 1916, before the age of 22, he went to work at Supermarine Aviation Works in Southampton, where he remained the rest of his life, serving as the Company Director for his last 10 years. Between 1922 and 1931, he designed seaplanes used largely for racing including the famous Schneider Cup Trophy, and by 1936, he had designed and developed the Spitfire that was known for its aerodynamic sleekness and build.

More than two dozen versions were eventually created before and after Mitchell's death. Every now and then, there comes along a man or a woman who seems to be able to change the course of history. The spitfire along with the hurricane and their very brave and courageous pilots went a long way to helping us turn the tide of events in the Second World War.

The Spitfire was a low-wing monoplane that was first flown in 1936 and was put into service with the Royal Air Force in 1938. It was modified continuously throughout the war to serve in a variety of roles including fighter with notable success at high altitudes, fighter-bomber, and photo-reconnaissance. The version that entered active service in 1938 had a top speed of about 360 miles *(580 km)* per hour and an armament of eight .303-inch machine guns. The Spitfire XIV, one of the last models of the war, had a ceiling of 40,000 feet *(12,200 m)* and a top speed of 440 miles *(710 km)* per hour; that version shot down more than 300 German V-1 missiles in 1944. When you think at that altitude it is around minus 45 degrees centigrade, flying a plane without a heater must have been on the fringe of survival – let alone trying to shoot down Germany's formidable weapons the V1 & V2 pilot-less missiles.

Sometimes in the winter, if you leave your car out at night there is an ice build-up on the windscreen. It is relatively easy to search for the de-ice spray; or for those who have forgotten to buy it, our plastic friend the credit card can be used as a scraper. Apart from the fact that there were no credit cards around in the old days, it would be mighty difficult to lean out of the window to scrape the windscreen of a plane, especially when there are a couple of Heinkels on your tail trying to blast you into eternity. Forget it if you need a pee, even if you really want to, you have to find your body part hidden in the depths of your clothing. Then finding the pee tube does not quite reach and besides which, it will be blocked with ice. However, that is probably the last thing on the pilot's mind; survival being the operative and paramount consideration. Truly, we need to be thankful for the exploits of our past heroes, who gave their lives in the name of freedom from tyranny and dictatorship. As the 2nd world war increased in intensity, the Spitfire's armament was increased to two 20-millimetre cannons along with two .50-inch machine guns or four .303-inch machine guns that made the plane a formidable flying tank. The last Spitfires in active service were used as photoreconnaissance planes with the Royal Air Force, and were retired in 1954, so the aircraft certainly got a lot of usage in both war and peacetime.

Fortunately today there are a great many Air Shows, notably in the USA and UK; so the post war generations can see flying in the sky where they belong the Spitfire with the Hurricane and a great many more old timers.

I spent many hours over the next couple of days probably getting in the way looking at the amazing machine and how it all went together. There were very few two-seat Spitfires built so it was very interesting to see this plane being restored to grace the skies once more. Anyway, it was at that moment I decided to start flying myself, having flown a little in a Chipmunk whilst in the Air Cadets, so the bug was already there. If anyone reading is from Guildford 261 squadron, a big hello! The Cadets is a great way to check out if the Royal Air Force is going to be for you when you grow up. From the RAF personnel to the internees and the great summer camps, I learnt a lot about comradeship and working as a team, which has helped me in later life.

The author in the centre by an RAF Chipmunk with Guildford 261 squadron air cadets. (photo by the flight instructor).

Even if you do not join the Air Force, being in the cadets is a wonderful experience. Sadly, some misguided doctor decided that I had flat feet and was therefore not allowed in the RAF. Although upsetting, as I dearly wanted to make the RAF my life, it was not to be; but flying small planes in many different parts of the northern hemisphere helped to make my dream come true.

Second (big) Hop By British Airways

A few years later, after obtaining my PPL *(private pilot's licence)* and going on to do my Commercial Licence and various add-on bits, I found myself sitting in the back of a British Airways 747. It was 1987 and I was with Denis en route to Miami where I was to collect his plane and ferry it back to the UK via Greenland.

However before departure, we had a problem at Heathrow Airport that was my fault entirely. Having a handgun in my flight bag did not go down too well with Security! It caused quite a stir at check in. Nevertheless, to carry such a weapon when travelling in the northern latitudes in case of a polar bear attack is quite normal. Especially if one should have the misfortune to make an emergency landing on an ice floe, where there just happened to be a hungry bear!

Showing my firearms certificate to Security did not change the attitude to this dilemma, but fortunately they relented when the BA aircrew said that they would look after the weapon until we were safely in Miami Airport. I have never bothered before, and after this fiasco it would be the first and last time that I intended to take a gun with me for a ferrying flight.

During the flight, I sat for a couple of hours in the jump seat in the cockpit of this ancient Jumbo. The visit to the flight deck was in the days before Terrorism crept into the world and sadly now keeps the cockpit closed. How many would-be pilots are deprived of the thrill of visiting the cockpit of the world's great airliners? It was good to see old-fashioned `steam` driven dials and no real electronics whatsoever in this early 747. Even the ancient green monochrome radar because of its size *(unlike the flat screen three-dimensional full colour vertical profile systems of today)* had to be mounted near the pilot and co-pilot's feet. It was quite funny when first going onto the flight deck because the co-pilot, whom I thought was doing up his shoelaces, was actually looking at the weather radar. Just do not ask what would happen if they both were looking down instead of out of the window!

It is quite amazing that pilots, regardless of the size or type of plane they fly, invariably talk incessantly about flying. We must be a pretty boring lot to non-aviation people!

Many airline crew still fly small aeroplanes for fun and recreation, and some hold awards for aerobatics! The passengers can be thankful that the captain or co-pilot up front is not going to do a loop-the-loop but merely contend themselves with button pushing and lever pulling and very importantly, bad weather watching! Pilots spend a lot of time both before and during flights planning the safest and least turbulent route.

It is generally taken for granted that planes can fly through any weather. This is a total fallacy – there are some seriously dangerous weather systems in the sky. It is the many years pilots spend training and studying that allows the passengers to relax, knowing that upfront there are two highly trained professional pilots looking after every person's welfare. Today, unlike years ago, it is possible to get satellite weather maps directly on the flat screen monitors in the cockpit. This gives real weather time and then superimposing the information on the route map helps the pilots, especially on long haul flights, to negotiate the weather ahead. Unlike a car one cannot change direction on a whim; there are too many aircraft in close proximity. Therefore a call to Air Traffic Control is required even mid ocean, and this can be time consuming – hence the importance of advance weather warnings.

On one trip in the UK flying back from Manchester to Fairoaks in the Company's Piper Seneca, Heathrow decided to `drop` me out of the airways above the beautiful spot of Henley-on-Thames; which is a fairly normal procedure. Henley being an appealing little town with the River Thames meandering through the centre and its ancient bridges straddling the water is always a pretty sight – though not that day. Heathrow were in the process of transferring me to Farnborough Air Traffic Control who would take over handling the remaining flight back to Fairoaks. The problem was the weather; with thunderstorms all around, looking at the radar screen was crucial. Suddenly Heathrow's parting comment was a shout; *"turn right immediately, incoming `heavy` (term for the large airliners) has made uncoordinated turn towards you, imperative you turn right immediately"!* My study of the Seneca's radar had been to avoid a very bright storm cell to my right; a bright blob that screamed at me to keep away! However, I had no choice but to turn into bad turbulence, and the gloom of heavy rain mixed with light hail, all because an airliner had turned without permission! Fortunately, a few minutes later descending through 5,000 feet the cloud turned into wispy shards of water-locked vapour, and tranquillity and normality came back into the flight. London Control Centre apologised and thanked me for my help. Evidently the airliner was getting a serious buffeting and to protect the passengers hanging on in the back, the pilot had to make the turn.

Back to the flight to Miami, high in the Stratosphere in the vast cockpit of the Jumbo some 38,000 feet above mother earth. The weather was more predictable and we had a glorious view of blue sky mixed with some high altitude cirrus cloud, with the ever-rolling waves of the North Atlantic beneath us. Quite a difference when flying light aircraft – you have to remain at a much lower level and are not able to escape bad weather. It does have its good points though, as the landscape is more distinct when the visibility is good.

Sadly, the 747 we were in has since been retired from active service, and is no doubt languishing in one of the many American desert resting places; along with all the other well-worn flying machines. It was one of British Airways first Jumbos and it had clocked up an incredible number of flights across the Atlantic. It goes to show what superb planes Boeing made and still make. In fact, the South African Captain, who was coincidently making one of his last flights before retirement, jokingly commented that although they had an Autopilot they never used it, as the plane knew the route so well it did not need one!

Coming into Miami is always exciting with such an amazing metropolis sprawled out on a very large flatland, with the Atlantic Ocean lapping on the sandy shores just a few yards from the buildings. Even before the aircraft door was open, people were excitedly getting ready to disembark into the electrifying and famous city.

Passing through the usual hustle and bustle of a major airport is invariably a hassle. The aircrew from our plane informed us that my piece of hand luggage was being put on the baggage carousel awaiting my collection. Not a good idea I thought, but hey this is America, and every man and his dog has a gun! At the conveyor belt, we were searching without success for my handgun in its locked holdall. I decided to call in the security officers who were quite concerned when I told them of the apparent missing weapon. Quickly several big guys turned up with radios blaring out unintelligible sounds, which I took to be a cross between Spanish and American. After a few minutes there was a shout from one of the security men, *"we have found your weapon"*. With many people giving us strange looks, I was re-united with my bag. It appeared that a police officer had noticed this brown holdall going around a carousel with a large orange label attached stating quite clearly *Firearm – Unloaded* and he wisely thought that he had better bring this item to the attention of the Customs office. The Customs were nonplussed as to why anyone would want to bring a gun into a country that has more guns than the population, which is a staggering 350 million *(people)*. Once I explained about not wanting to become bear bait, which I might well without a gun, we left the red declaration zone with the Custom guys muttering something about there being no polar bears in Florida and have a nice day.

Hop Around Florida

Wally Evans, my aircraft broker met us at the arrivals area and whisked us away in his mammoth Lincoln Continental. Sitting in the back of the car, which had enough room for a small dance floor, I started thinking about the trip. I had flown for Denis part-time for several years and we were doing some contract work for a mapping agency. Their sole purpose in life was to photograph and map the motorways and towns in the UK. Today satellite imagery tends to replace the aerial photographer, but without that personal touch. Only people can do special oblique photos and high quality images, and undertaking this work was tremendous fun. Denis, who used to sit in the back with a monster camera attached to the floor that took several hundred images on one spool, was always good entertainment. That was apart from the odd times when he shouted at me for not turning quickly enough or flying a slightly incorrect heading.

He had his eye on a twin-engine plane to complement his already ancient Cessna 182, a 4-seat high wing single engine beast which had the temperament of a water buffalo yet did the required job. Whenever he talked about the twin he had a sparkle in his eyes, but they must have clouded over when eventually we came face to face with what appeared to be a derelict plane; which in fact was a derelict plane! However, once he had set his mind on something there was no going back, and the rules of flying over London were quite clear – two engines or not allowed. Denis had been awarded a lucrative contract to photograph the M25, and more importantly central London, so a twin-engine plane was an urgent requirement. Helicopters are great for the odd London job, but they are very expensive to operate, and can have problems with vibration. Denis also had some work at sea, filming oilrigs in action. The thought of flying the antique single engine Cessna over the stormy and icy wastes of the North Sea at low level did not bear thinking about.

Having brought a conventional twin engine plane back from Miami for my Company a few months earlier, Denis thought that I would be a suitable candidate to export this twin-engine plane from the USA to London. Unfortunately, the Cessna 336 was an old relic from the Vietnam War. During that campaign the might of the American War Machine had chosen a batch of 336`s to be used as aerial machine-gun back-up planes.

The main advantage for Denis of the 336, was that the engines were not on the wings as with conventional twin-engine planes, but had one in the front, and the other fitted to the rear of the fuselage. It also had fixed undercarriage instead of the normal retractable type. This was ideal for making holes in the floor and removing windows. With no engines or undercarriage to get in the way it was perfect for photography. The later more modern and comfortable Cessna 337 Skymaster with retractable undercarriage, of which some models were even pressurised, was not suitable, *(see photo on page 52).*

There were twin tail booms to support the elevator and rudder – an idea taken from post war British fighters the De Havilland Vampire and the Sea Venom. The downside with this engine arrangement was that the poor people who sat in this machine were effectively between two large 6-cylinder engines, and as you can imagine, the noise was terrible. It had been known for the inexperienced pilot to take off with just the front engine running - such was the racket - and unless an eye was kept on the engine instruments this could easily happen.

Clyde Vernon Cessna worked as a farmhand, a prospector, a threshing-machine operator, and an automobile salesman until he saw a flying circus in Oklahoma and decided to be a flyer. He worked at an airplane factory in the Bronx, New York City, for two months and then returned to Oklahoma where he flew his first plane in 1911.

Looking at the 336 you can understand how Clyde as a farmhand maybe had dreams of making a flying tractor! In 1917 he produced a monoplane powered by a 6-cylinder air-cooled engine. In the 1920's he joined forces with businessman and air enthusiast Victor Roos to produce Cessna-Roos aircraft until 1927. Then Cessna bought out the Company, which was closed *(1931-34)* during the Great Depression. Cessna retired in 1934. A revived Cessna Aircraft Company later became one of the world's largest manufacturers of private airplanes. In 1992 the Company was acquired by Textron Inc. that still builds most of the models, but most definitely not the Cessna 336.

However, the military would not care about a very noisy plane, and the war was long over when Cessna stopped making the 336. The military advantage was that with a high wing and no engines to get in the way they could mount a machine gun inside the cabin and point it out through the doorway. In addition, the fixed undercarriage was strong and perfect for landing on dusty airstrips.

The noise that this unusually designed aircraft makes inside the plane, especially with the door removed, defies belief *(something that I found out when doing special photo work)*. Needless to say, the military left most of them in Vietnam after the war, as it would not have been cost effective to bring every remaining plane back to the States. You could almost hear America breathe a deep sigh of relief knowing that many of these rowdy machines were left languishing in Vietnam. No doubt the local Vietnamese farmers found many uses for them, including pig and chicken shelters. I would have thought that the 336 would make a good crop duster, but I never heard of one ever being used for that particular role.

The Cessna 336 that Denis bought – one engine in the front and the other behind – least it was when we took off! The early models of this 6 seat plane had no room for luggage had a drab colour scheme, and was not very successful. Later models had a strap-on hold put beneath the fuselage, and improved paint work (photo by author).

The Vietnam War had therefore left a shortage in America of this type of plane. Though odd ones were still for sale, they were hard to find, and quite often in bad condition. The residents of central Florida must have been mighty pleased upon hearing through the grapevine that a crazy Englishman had bought the last remaining Cessna 336 in Florida, and was about to attempt to fly it back to England. The plane was not really too bad; it did fly ok and was simple enough, but as with the majority of light aircraft it was extremely loud. The large turbo engines had no exhaust system whatsoever. That was a major problem in designing light aircraft – nobody seemed capable of making an exhaust system which would quieten the engine down to an acceptable level. To add misery to 336 passengers and the pilot, the engines were in tandem, causing harmonic disturbances from the propeller air turbulence hitting the wings and the 2 tail fins.

Denis had located the plane at Opa-Locka Airport in North Miami after many telephone calls and a subsequent inspection trip by the broker. It had been unloved, untouched, and probably forgotten if it wasn't for Denis stirring someone's memory. Many people when buying something, regardless of what they are purchasing, tend to get enthusiastically carried away with the dream, and perhaps do not put in enough thought and research prior to the deal. For many years this plane had been sheltering under one of the large leafed moss covered trees that you find in Florida, with clinging dark green ivy hanging off the branches. It gave the impression that Jurassic Park is still with us; it only needed Tarzan to come swinging on the vines to complete the picture.

Apart from looking rather forlorn, the plane seemed to have become a perfect location for scorpions, snakes, and black widow spiders *(all venomous)*. A Zoo might be a better place to get a closer look at the various species that were living in this abandoned machine. I am rather squeamish, and the thought of any of these still hiding in the plane when we eventually took to the air made me shudder. A bite whilst flying could have very ignominious consequences to my flying career.

The engineer who was cautiously standing a few paces behind assured us that it would be ready in a couple of weeks; he was obviously a man with a sense of humour. However, the maintenance organisation started to work on the machine with a lot of enthusiasm; bits and pieces were taken off and then put back, hopefully in the proper order.

Bearing in mind that Spring was on the horizon, Florida started getting unbearably hot. When we started test flying it was done in such high humidity that after landing it was like walking straight out of a shower with all your clothes on. Forget what you see on the films with the pilot walking across the tarmac with his smart uniform and cleanly pressed white shirt. In those temperatures we ended up looking like a couple of refugees who had just swum across the sea, soaking wet and feeling extremely yucky.

The Cessna 337 (the good model) – the high speed pressurised version with retractable undercarriage and improved engines. Even though it was pressurised, it still could not quite make it out of the Troposphere. However, the plane could cruise above most bad weather, and was much better to fly than the 336. (file photo)

The airport was located in North Miami and was more settled and peaceful than Miami City centre. I got to know a great Cuban Restaurant in the local area just by the airport. Main lunch of the day being pan-fried fresh snapper, boiled rice, diced banana, and black re-fried beans. I can thoroughly recommend that dish and like so many ethnic restaurants, the people were very friendly and always had time for a chat.

The local sheriff complete with six-gun and badge used to frequent the eating-house at lunch times. I exchanged many good yarns with this friendly peacekeeper, mine from the UK, and his tales of desperados and chasing bandits in the U.S. Somehow, I felt that he was living a hundred years too late and maybe the Wyatt Earp and Billy the Kid era would have suited him better. Mind you, if you bounced into him there was every chance that you would ricochet off the walls of the café just like that scene in Star Wars where Han Solo fired his laser gun at the monster in the garbage hold on the evil empires battleship: such was the sheriff's build.

One day it was a little embarrassing when he got up to leave. His tummy rolled along the table following his body. However, he forgot that at the end of the seat was an elbow bar covered in cheap PVC, presumably to stop you falling out of your cubicle. Part of his handcuffs caught on the end of the bar and there was a loud ripping sound. Without going into too much detail, his trousers ripped open in his haste to extricate himself from the seat. I did what any decent person would do, and yelled after him, *"don't worry about paying as you have enough problems, so I will treat you to your lunch"*. With a grunt of thanks, he tried his best to make a dignified exit. This could only happen in America!

Spectacular view of Miami Skyline courtesy Miami Convention Bureau.

Many people say that Florida is flat and not particularly attractive, and whilst they would to a point be correct, there is more to this famous state than meets the eye. It is a little like an enormous iceberg, but a very hot one, floating in a semi fluid state. The whole eco system is in a fragile condition and the very high influx of people moving into Florida does nothing to alleviate the situation. However, it does have its own unique charm and having spent a few years there on a semi-permanent basis, I found the people friendly, very polite and extremely helpful whether in the aviation sector or just in the street. It is certainly true that you can fly across the state *(which is pretty much the size of England)* at 100 feet and only have to avoid the odd crane, billboard, tennis or golf ball that may just happen to get in your way.

Even more astounding is the fact that you can fly at that height from Florida Keys up to North Carolina and beyond, a distance of some 1,600 miles plus, and remain intact in your plane. That distance would equate with flying from Norway down towards the Mediterranean – and there you would be lucky to travel more than a few miles without bumping into something hard! OK, so there are a few other places in the world which are pretty flat, i.e. the Sahara Desert, the world's oceans and East Anglia in the UK but they're certainly not so exciting as the East Coast of the USA.

Florida is very reasonable on costs compared to England. Denis was to find out just how reasonable when comparing living costs later in Greenland and Iceland. They are without doubt amongst the most costly places on earth. Talking of expenditure, Wally's Lincoln Continental was one of the largest cars in the States. The fuel consumption alone would bankrupt you in the UK, and certainly the car would not fit on little old England's roads. Although Wally had an office at Opa-Locka Airport, he managed to keep his filing cabinet in the trunk of his gargantuan beast, along with his tools and various bits and pieces.

There is a map on the next page showing our route from Miami in the south, along a gentle curve up through Georgia and the Carolinas to Virginia.

56

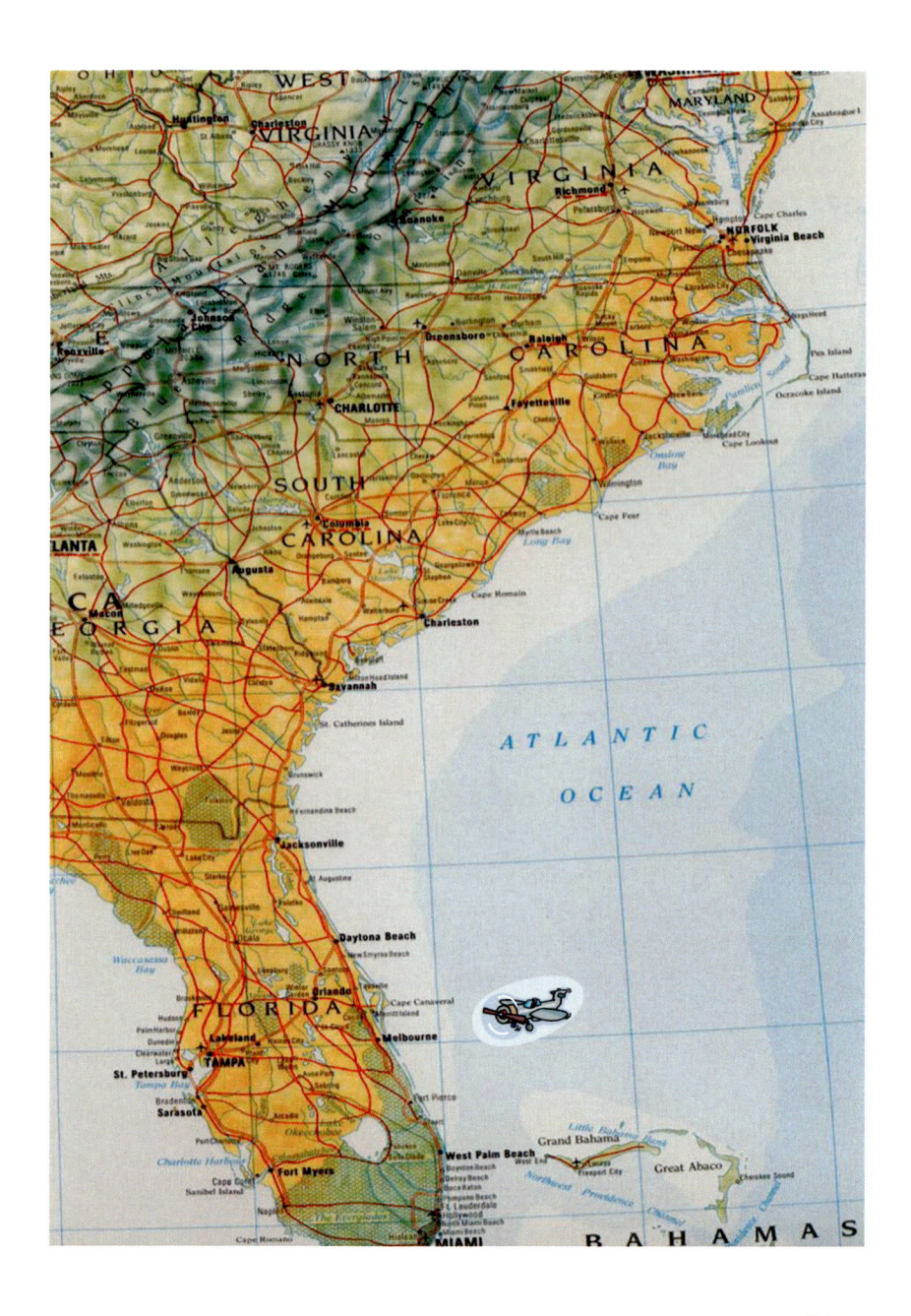

Alligator On The Runway

Well it happens! Especially in Florida. Wally Evans the broker, apart from buying and selling aircraft, ran a small cargo service around South Florida and the Caribbean. He had a delivery to Everglade City Airport to drop off some fresh supplies to an Expedition in `gator` territory. I did not need much persuading when asked if I would make the trip. I got into an old twin engine Piper Seneca One that I had used in the past for various deliveries for Wally around Florida. This model can bite the unwary, as if one engine fails, the only thing the plane does is to go down giving you a 50% increase in engine failure. Unless the `extra` engine can keep you flying a twin-engine plane is a liability in confidence. The Seneca One was a badly designed low powered machine with very heavy rudder controls and has scant comparison with the later models. The latest much-improved Seneca proved to be a very popular entry-level training aeroplane into the more complex types of passenger aircraft.

Still for a 90 minute round trip to Everglade City, it did not matter, and besides I had the `gator` to contend with! The Everglades are unique and quite irreplaceable, but are unfortunately full of aggressive alligators and many nasty snakes. During my numerous flights in Florida, every time my flight took me over the swamplands in a single engine plane, I would keep a sharp look out for somewhere safe to land just in case the engine should fail. Visual navigation *(map reading)* around Florida was quite easy - most roads are straight and there are no major roads in south central Florida, apart from the famous `Alligator Alley`. This links the Gulf coast to Miami and the Atlantic in a cross-country direction. It is the route favoured by pilots in slow flying single engine planes – giving them a fighting chance of survival should the engine quit. Being close to a road rather than an emergency landing in the middle of swamp was far more preferable *(though alligators might not agree with me)*. The railway tracks were another favourite navigation aid; usually trains loaded with fruit were criss-crossing the land and were easy to locate.

Arriving 2,000 feet overhead the airport with Everglade City *(not a city at all but a small township)* partly hidden in the mangroves, I could not help but to be in awe of the beautiful view of the Florida Everglades. Stretching out before me with the colours from an artist's palette, a tranquil blue sky, contrasting lush green of the mangrove trees, a bright yellow sandy beach and the deep blue waters of the Gulf of Mexico - it was a view to remember.

A gentle turn over the surf rolling onto the beach, I received clearance to land from the airport Controller who just happened to be sipping a morning coffee in the pilot lounge (*a regular occurrence in small airfields*). She warned me that there was a small alligator basking in the rising heat on the concrete taxiway and to proceed with caution. She sounded more concerned about the alligator than my welfare. I cleared the runway and passed the `gator` with a few feet to spare. He or she had obviously not warmed up enough as there was barely a movement, and it showed a total lack of interest in either the plane or me. Having said that, had the alligator decided to open his mouth wide and show me his teeth, there was every chance that he would have got a mouthful of propeller that might have rearranged his molars a little!

The bushes of the everglades along the taxiway occasionally brushed the starboard wing tip, so close were the swamplands. Stopping in front of a small reception area, I dropped off the cardboard boxes full of food for the expedition along with some medical equipment, and a small generator which presumably would enable them to move around after dark. With a quick turnaround and with the gator having been persuaded by several determined staff to return to the undergrowth, I took off saying goodbye to the tower as the undercarriage wound itself back into the wings and the plane was once more in its element. Overflying the airport the expedition party who were delving into the boxes waved to me as they loaded the contents onto a one of those very noisy airboats that you see so often in the swamplands. Looking down upon the thousands of orange groves that seem to cover Florida I flew a diagonal course across the rows, and from an event free trip to Everglade City I returned to Opa-Locka. After parking the Seneca, I was pleased to see a little more progress had been made on the Cessna at the engineer's workshop. As evening was drawing on, Denis and I returned to our hotel that was in the famous Miami Lakes Golf Complex. Despite the fact that neither of us played golf, it was undoubtedly a pleasant place to be. There was the added pleasure of an evening walk, and kicking the odd misplaced golf ball into one of the many small lakes.

Wally lived in a well-established local community near the hotel and it was a delight to visit him in the evening. It was a small friendly environment where people knew each other even though surrounded by a large city. His favourite place was the local eating-house, complete with multi-coloured settees and an old juke box in the corner, still a dime a record. The low mounted coffee tables were just the place to put your feet up relax and chat with the residents. Just think of some of the funny American sit coms on television and you have it being re-enacted in Wally's local cafe,

Next to the airport, there is a memorial park dedicated to Amelia Earhart *(1898–1937)*, the US aviator and first woman to fly solo across the Atlantic in 1932. In 1937, she attempted to fly around the world, but tragically disappeared in the Pacific Ocean July 2, en route from Lae, New Guinea to Howland Island in the Pacific. A true pioneer in every sense of the word. Having time to spare I did a little research. Denis was by his beloved plane egging on the mechanics so I visited the Memorial Park. Apart from being a very famous aviator, she was also a wealthy and beautiful socialite. Therefore, I thought it was appropriate to remember one of the world's great women pioneers.

Amelia was in many ways far more famous than Charles Lindbergh, whose epic single engine transatlantic crossing in `The Spirit of St Louis` a few years earlier than Amelia's made all the headlines. Lindbergh crossed the Atlantic in 1927, fantastic if you realise that 23 years earlier no plane was flying – only a distant dream. When she was 10 years old Amelia Mary Earhart saw her first plane at a State Fair: she was not impressed. *"It was a thing of rusty wire and wood and looked not at all interesting,"* she said. It was not until she attended a stunt-flying exhibition, almost a decade later that she became seriously interested in aviation. A pilot spotted Amelia and her friend, who were watching from an isolated clearing, and dived at them. I am sure he said to himself, `Watch me make them scarper`. Amelia stood her ground as the plane swooped by and something inside her awakened.

61

"I did not understand it at the time," she said, *"but I believe that little red airplane said something to me as it swished by."* On December 28, 1920, pilot Frank Hawks gave her a ride that would forever change her life. *"By the time I had got two or three hundred feet off the ground,"* she said *"I knew I had to fly".*

Although her convictions were strong, financial and prejudicial obstacles awaited her. The former tomboy was no stranger to disapproval or doubt and took life in big strides. Defying conventional feminine behaviour, the young Earhart climbed trees, `belly-slammed` her sledge to start it downhill and hunted rats with a .22 rifle. She also kept a scrapbook of newspaper clippings about successful women in predominantly male-oriented fields, including film direction, production, law, advertising, management, and mechanical engineering. After graduating from Hyde Park High School in 1915, she worked as a nurse's aide in a military hospital in Canada during WWI, attended college, and later became a social worker.

She took her first flying lesson on January 3, 1921, and in six months managed to save enough money to buy her first plane. The second-hand Kinner Airster was a two-seater biplane painted bright yellow. Amelia named the plane `Canary` and used it to set her first women's record by rising to an altitude of 14,000 feet. Only a few years previously, 3,000 feet was considered high. She was in fact way ahead of the competition including Charles Lindberg; this at a time when women were still considered the *underdog*. She proved to a lot of people just how capable the female was becoming. Amelia opened many doors for numerous other women who wanted to break free of the old ideology. She must have been sympathetic to Mrs Emily Pankhurst, the suffragette in London, who at the turn of the century (1903-1906) fought so hard for women's liberation.

One afternoon in April 1928, a personal phone call came for her at work. *"I'm too busy to answer just now,"* she said. After hearing that it was important, she took the call. At first she thought it was someone playing a prank, but when the caller convinced her he was serious in asking her *"Would you like to fly the Atlantic?"* Earhart promptly replied, *"Yes!"* After an interview in New York with the project coordinators, including book publisher and publicist George P. Putnam, she was asked to join pilot Wilmer `Bill` Stultz and co-pilot/mechanic Louis E. `Slim` Gordon. The team left Trepassey harbour, Newfoundland, in a Fokker F7 named Friendship on June 17, 1928, and arrived at Bury Port, Wales, 21 hours later.

This was barely a year after Charles Lindbergh's epic flight. Their landmark flight made headlines worldwide, and when the crew returned to the United States, they were greeted with a ticker-tape parade in New York and a reception held by President Calvin Coolidge at the White House. Yet this was not a single person flight, the fuss was because there had been a woman on board!

From then on, Amelia Earhart's life revolved around flying. She was placed third at the Cleveland Women's Air Derby; later nicknamed the `Powder Puff Derby` by Will Rogers. As fate would have it, her life also began to include George Putnam. The two developed a friendship during preparation for the Atlantic crossing and were married February 7, 1931. Intent on retaining her independence, she referred to the marriage as a `partnership` with `dual control` Together they worked on secret plans for Amelia to make a solo flight across the Atlantic. On May 20, 1932, she started the trek from Grace Harbour, Newfoundland, to Paris. Strong north winds, icy conditions, and mechanical problems plagued the flight and forced her to land in a pasture near Londonderry, Ireland. After scaring most of the cows in the neighbourhood, she pulled up in a farmer's back yard.

As word of her flight spread, the media surrounded her, both overseas and in the United States. President Herbert Hoover presented Amelia Earhart with a gold medal from the National Geographic Society. Congress awarded her the Distinguished Flying Cross; the first ever given to a woman. At the ceremony, Vice President Charles Curtis praised her, saying she displayed *"heroic courage and skill as a navigator at the risk of her life"*. Amelia felt the flight proved that men and women were equal in jobs requiring intelligence, coordination, speed, coolness and willpower. The Disappearance of Amelia Earhart by Gordon Theisen is one of the books that I can thoroughly recommend to discover more about this amazing intrepid aviator.

Back to the story of my little hops, which in no way could ever match the many who have gone before; brave adventurous pioneers such as Amelia Earhart, Beryl Markham, Jean Batten, Ernest Gann, Charles Lindbegh, Richard Byrd, Wiley Post and others who paved the way for our modern world. Al Stewart the famous singer, dedicated the hit song *flying sorcery* to the British pioneer Amy Johnson who flew virtually around the world single-handed during the early 1930`s.

Between the World Wars was a most exciting period in aviation history. Almost daily pilots were breaking speed and distance records, designers were revolutionizing aircraft design, and manufacturers were building more and better planes. Barnstormers, air shows, and flying circuses fascinated the public and drew large crowds. Oceans and continents were conquered, even Howard Hughes in 1938 *(the future reclusive billionaire)*, with four companions circumnavigated the globe in record time, 3 days, 19 hours. No one had done that since Wiley Post five years before.

Safety was at last appearing on the scene, and happily parachute design dramatically improved during the First World War, and as such, saved the lives of many pilots flying crazy stunts with such fragile planes. The earliest parachute goes back to the 1700's - a long time before aeroplanes - being something like a bed sheet, with the four corners having a knotted rope joining a few feet below. The first to try the jump was in fact, a poor hapless dog. In 1785 he was thrown out of an air balloon by his owner, and happily, he survived. In the early days there was a less than a 50% chance of a parachute opening correctly, but at least it was a start.

Sadly many brave fliers set out to fly long distances and simply disappeared; usually swallowed up without a trace in the oceans. It still happens, I knew of two pilots flying together from Greenland to Iceland, each in a single engine plane. Only one made it the other tragically disappearing beneath the icy waters. Ferry flying small single engine planes is dangerous in these inhospitable regions. The survivor was Brian the person who subsequently was to fly Denis's 336 back to the UK.

Some aircraft manufacturers have now brought out a couple of single engine planes with ballistic parachutes. In the event of an engine failure or something else equally serious, the hapless pilot can pull a lever enabling a parachute to open on the top of the fuselage, and both plane and pilot can descend in safety. That is providing what lies underneath you is survivable after landing! However it is still a brilliant idea and has to make flying a little safer. The idea actually came from the early astronaut days when space capsules returning to Earth, with the heroic astronauts inside, were suspended beneath giant parachutes, to facilitate the descent.

A Short Hop -The Wrong Way

Back to the other side of the fence, I was getting a little fed up with waiting for the Cessna 336 to be made flyable. An engineer who was nicknamed *`the smoking mechanic`* was repairing Denis's plane. I might add that the `smoking mechanic` was a retired Spanish engineer who used to maintain Boeing 707's in the Canary Islands. He was so called because he always had a cigarette hanging out of his mouth, sometimes alight and sometimes just smouldering. I was amazed that he had managed to live this long without blowing up both himself and a plane. Rolling back his sleeves, being the only person in Florida with a long sleeved shirt, he hitched up his oily jeans, parked his cigarette behind his ear, as would a carpenter with a pencil, and commenced work. Being in let-us-keep-living mode, I retired to the little coffee bar next door in the Flying Club. Here I could watch the plane being repaired, camera ever ready to catch any action, and be far enough away to survive should a fire erupt at the end of the mechanic's cigarette and engulf Denis's Cessna in the ensuing fireball. To amuse themselves some of the instructors at the

Club were taking bets on how long the mechanic's luck would last before they had to call out the fire brigade. It has been known that on occasions a sudden yell in unintelligible Spanish would confirm that the offending item was still lit when placed in its `parking spot`. What would the world be without these characters? A safer place I hear you cry.

We were located, or perhaps marooned would be a better word, in the less salubrious part of the airport. Most of the little maintenance buildings were host to planes in various states of decomposition, but it felt like home to me, having always dreamed of owning my own aircraft junk yard. You can laugh but some of the relics I've flown should have really been put in a scrap yard.

Meanwhile, Wally had found me another flying job to deliver down to the Dominican Republic a very small two seat Cessna 152 Aerobat. Over the years I had delivered several aircraft around the Florida peninsula for him and I looked forward to a change of scenery. The 152 is an extremely basic aerobatic plane, slightly more robust than the Cessna 150, and was needed for a flying school situated in the capital. It meant two night stopovers, one in Exuma Island, South Bahamas, where I was to drop off some equipment for Wally, and another in the beautiful islands of Turks & Caicos.

Flying a slow single engine plane through the West Indies/Caribbean sounds beautiful and believe me it is a dream come true. The only difficulty was that with nowhere to put in a ferry tank, fuel versus distance was a problem, and meant making several stops en route.

A vertical view of Opa-Locka Airport, North Miami - as big as most major European Airports but without terminal buildings (file photo).

With the warm waters being prolific with sharks, stingrays, and big Manta rays, I did not want to run out of fuel half way between islands. When I say that the Cessna 150`s and 152`s are small, I mean `really` small. At least without a passenger there was enough room for my trusty liferaft. Even in these warm seas, you need somewhere to go whilst waiting to be rescued in the event of a ditching, and swimming around was obviously out of the question.

Today's modern light aircraft are fitted, in the name of economy, with very small engines. The aircraft are by definition `light` which means there is little place to put in large fuel tanks. Besides which, too much fuel means no surplus load capacity to carry people and luggage. The upside is that the plane would probably float if you ditch in fairly calm waters, a low wing being preferable to a high wing plane, as you can just step out, and sit relaxing on the wing. Otherwise, in the high wing after ditching, you need to wait until the cockpit fills with water before you can open the door. The pressure of water has to equalise both outside and inside. It takes some nerve to sit patiently in the seat whilst the plane is filling up with water going over your head, and possibly sinking. You have to be careful not to inflate the lifejacket until clear of the plane. It would be disastrous when the moment came to leave the plane if you found that the item meant to save your life is actually preventing your exit! There were some Cessna aircraft such as the Cessna 150, 152 and the 172 which were built with a quick release door that would make an escape a lot easier.

Bahamas Hop

Emptying my mind of such thoughts and after a normal take off from Opa-Locka airport, I headed southeast in the little Cessna 152. Keeping well clear of Fort Lauderdale and Miami international Airports, I aimed for Bimini, the first island eastward from Miami and first in the chain of Bahamian Islands. Flying over calm seas, Bimini appeared on the horizon, the sandy isthmus joining the two small islands. The sea's gentle shelving revealing an assortment of rocks and seaweed in the clear waters. Coming into land, you actually fly over the wreckage of an old twin engine DC3. Having tried to land at night without lights it did not quite make the runway, and lies in the clear waters of the lagoon by the airport. I might add that the plane was carrying a cargo of drugs at the time and it was quite a common occurrence to see a plane in such a state. Rather an ignoble end to one of the most successful aircraft ever made. These planes were being built before the start of the Second World War, so it goes to show how well they were constructed. Even today, there are still quite a few DC3's and DC4's flying around.

Ma Cox ran the café at Bimini Airport and I could not believe it when a very friendly black buxom lady announced her name. The cafe was the usual ramshackle of corrugated iron roofs *(partly rusty red),* half-opened windows, an interior painted in a mixture of vibrant colours, and an old `Rock-Ola` music box in the corner. Calypso music was playing quietly in the background, competing with the whirr of the air conditioning unit which was doing its best to keep the room cool. I sat on an amply cushioned bamboo chair set before a rickety bamboo table. Whilst I consumed an early lunch of red snappers and the ever-available fried chips, Ma Cox and I had a great conversation, trying to establish a family connection between us; but we could not find a link.

Life in this part of the world is a much laid-back affair, and it was delightful to spend a little while in such picturesque surroundings. From the small airport it was a short walk through some green ferns onto the golden sands and the sea. One of the best diving and fishing places around, scuba divers come to Bimini from all over the world for reef and wreck diving. With its crystal clear waters and gentle currents it truly is a superb area for all water sports.

After a stimulating stroll I returned to the airport and said goodbye to Ma Cox. She gave me a hug that would flatten a sumo wrestler, and we parted company; or to be more precise I extricated myself from her grip!

One day I will return to that island and visit Bonefish Hole, Porgy Bay, and the shipwrecks with Spanish gold; and once again sample Ma Cox's hospitality. Sadly, Bimini, like so many other beautiful locations, has now become overburdened with buildings and tourists and has lost some of its original old world charm. It is a pity that modernisation makes such detrimental changes to unique islands like Bimini.

Waiting in a very hot aeroplane, and starting to melt from the sun bearing down on me, I received clearance from the Air Traffic Controller. He was in fact having a large cold drink in Ma Cox's bar, and chatted to me over his portable transmitter as he bade me farewell. When small airstrips have no Controller on duty, pilots merely use a Unicom frequency giving blind calls as to their position and intentions. That way, other pilots could assess the caller's proximity to their own location and with safety foremost in mind, with a certain amount of courtesy, they would follow one another landing or taking off.

Lining up on the runway, which was a little potholed, and with grass breaking through the joins in the concrete, I pointed due east, took off over the crystal clear waters and thought to myself – I want to live here – it is like going to heaven but staying on earth. But then, even paradise can get a little monotonous, and I was looking forward to my further adventures. Though maybe, just maybe, if I suddenly became rich, I would not need too much arm-twisting to settle down with a boat in the harbour, a plane at the airport, and a beach house with a happy family in between!

Next hop of about 120 miles from beautiful Bimini was to the tourist area of The Grand Bahamas. Not a place I could rave about, especially after landing at Nassau International with its immensely long runway to accommodate the large Boeing 747 aircraft bringing in the tourists.

Coming from the peace of Bimini it was quite a revelation the difference from one island to another. Nassau Airport being so large it was a half-mile walk in the searing sun to the Customs post for my passport to be stamped and to fill out lots of forms, even though I had recently cleared Customs in Bimini. I probably had enough fuel to have made Great Exuma in one hit, but with no rush it was interesting dropping in various places en-route.

Filling a high wing plane with petrol wherever you are was an art in itself. It meant standing on a piece of bent aluminium half way up the wing strut, leaning over the top of the wing to open the fuel cap, and then looking around hopefully for the person behind who would hand up the nozzle of the hose. Once the tank was full, everything was done in reverse to get back on the ground and then repeated on the other wing. Occasionally there were refuel trucks with a pair of small steps, which made the job a lot easier and safer.

Filing a flight plan that had to have a London GMT on the form was rather ridiculous, as this gave a departure time of some 9 hours difference to the local time. I learnt from other pilots that when advising an arrival time it varied from `be there soon` to `will arrive later`. I hope that the Heathrow Air Traffic Controllers are reading this!

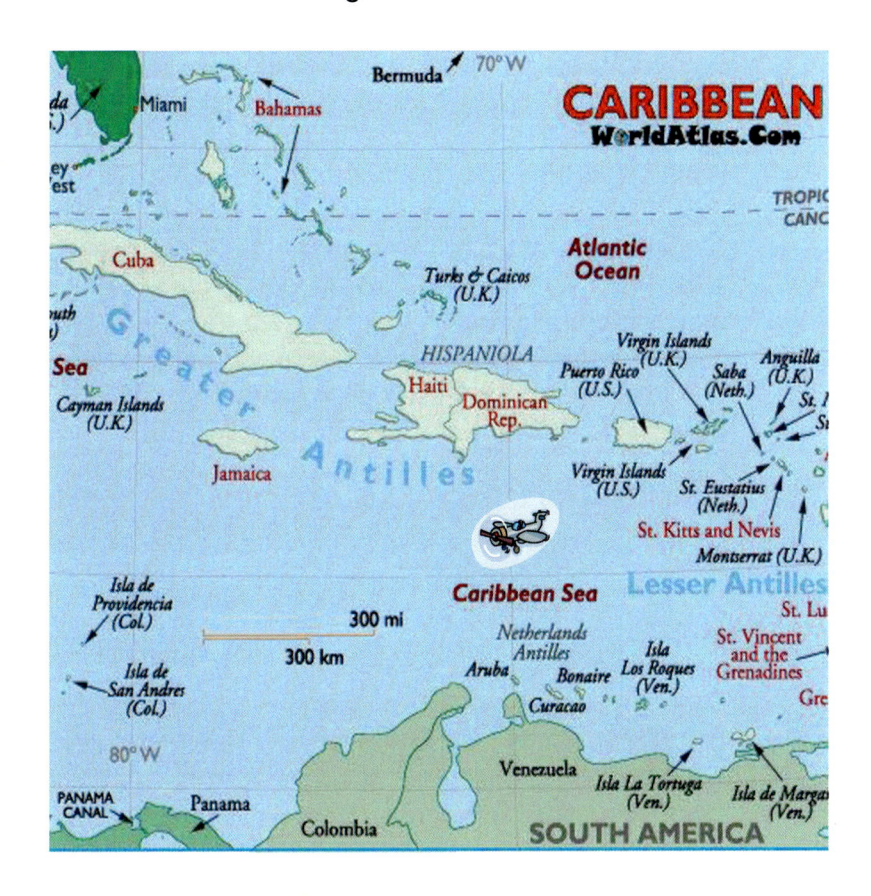

Map courtesy of worldatlas.com

I think it prudent to mention that any pilot flying in the West Indies/Caribbean needs to buy the `flying bible`.

It is called `Bahamas Pilot & Caribbean Aviation Guide` and is an informative book describing in great detail all the islands except, strangely enough, the Dominican Republic; though in later editions this error was rectified. This book lists all that the budding aviation person, and anyone else for that matter, wanted from a truly informative guide. It is interesting to know a few key facts about this archipelago of Islands. There are believed to be 700 islands and 2,000 or so smaller islets in the Caribbean from Florida down to South America. That sounds like an awful lot of rocks sticking up out of the water and I wonder who actually went around this idyllic part of the world and counted them all? Though let's face it, wouldn't you like the job? Something that I have always tried to understand is when does a rock become an island: in a similar way to when does a boat become a ship? Size I hear you say – but then who decides what size is small and what size is big?

The islets are locally known as Cays and are often owned by private individuals, and many of them do not want any form of intrusion. They will put large oil drums or rocks across the airstrips of the larger islets thus preventing anyone from landing. If that does not put them off then it is not unknown for shots to be fired, presumably not directly at the hapless pilot!

Apart from the few Cays with dubious owners, the majority of the Caribbean is quite a paradise for everyone. However one always has to be extremely cautious of the drug problem and never to accept mysterious parcels that need `*dropping off*` in Miami. In addition, it is wise to firmly lock a plane and prior to departure check around extremely carefully to see if anything has been moved. It may seem like something out of a James Bond movie – but the penalties are severe for smuggling, and the Customs may not believe you are innocent. Sticking a piece of special tape across all the doors works wonders, as the tape can never be replaced without one noticing something is amiss.

A pretty important point when you think of it is the weather. Whilst the sun shines, it can get mighty hot and there can be some pretty furious weather systems anytime of the year, but especially from May to September. The latter part of summer can produce severe hurricanes or storms of such magnitude that even large passenger planes can be destroyed or severely damaged. Therefore you can imagine what nature can do to little planes! Without weather radar, which my little Cessna would not even have room for, I had to make sure that I stayed in visual contact with the ground, or in my case the sea.

In the summer there are the inevitable thunderstorms, and though of fairly short duration and local in size, they have to be avoided at all costs. Thunderstorms are quite lazy, and the early morning riser can often make a flight in the smoothest of air. It is mid afternoon, with a build up of humidity, when the avid aviator has to keep his/her eyes well open for the developing Cumulonimbus cloud *(CB)*.The rising heat would awake from its from slumber, ready to reach out and encompass the unwary aviator in a very turbulent, dark blanket of cloud. Yet another hazard ready to trap the unsuspecting are the waterspouts; whilst not so common as thunderstorms they do exist. Normally they are visible, though you need to keep your eyes well open for this phenomenon. If you see dark heavy moisture laden clouds at a few thousand feet with even darker `*udders*` forming a suspended pendulous form beneath them, this is classic waterspout weather running from the bottom of the cloud to the sea below or vice versa.

With my head in the clouds as it so often is, *(pardon the pun)* I set off in the late afternoon for Georgetown in Great Exuma Island, where an evening meal and a bed were waiting. Leaving Nassau and keeping a weather eye open for the thunderstorms building up, I flew down past Andros the largest island in the Bahamas Chain. It's around 100 miles long by 40 miles wide. Andros is probably best known and world famous for `*Bone Fishing*`. Evidently, these fish are extremely elusive to catch and any fisherman who needs a challenge will go Bone fishing. You have to be dedicated, as other than fishing, there appears little else to do on the island; apart from maybe writing books. Passing over Cat Island, with the sun setting in a blaze of glorious red, heralding a fine day for tomorrow, a descending turn over the island of San Salvador put me on track for the runway. With Rum Cay beneath my wings in an ocean of blue, I made the final approach over the ramshackle marina into Georgetown, Great Exuma Island.

After landing on the airstrip, I checked in with Customs. Although still officially in the Bahamas the drug problem is always in the background, and coming from Nassau, a very rich and commercial part of the Bahamian chain, to Exuma, always attracts the Customs. You have to see to it to believe the couple of ramshackle buildings that were the Immigration and Customs Control offices. They were made of wood and brick with old rusty corrugated iron roofs, and windows without any glass. A few chickens pecking at the odd patches of grass completed the scene; it was like something out of a 1940`s movie. I hope they never change the old world look of the place.

Just a few feet away was the airport snack bar that had a large veranda with tables underneath the awning, and music blaring out in the traditional Bahamian style. Strangely enough, there is more chicken on the menu than fish – come to think of it, chicken was the only dish on the menu! Presumably chicken is easier to keep and cook, and in my case would be easier to catch as I am the world's worst fisherman; besides which, the best fresh fish goes north to the restaurants in Nassau and Miami.

Tucking the Cessna 152 for the night in a corner of the airstrip, a little rest, a cup of coffee. I then made my way down to the harbour, which had a marina of sorts - wooden posts hammered into the seabed with a rickety wooden jetty between them. It was a little nostalgic, as I remembered the last time when staying here with Wally in his little corner of paradise. I looked over to the old hotel where we had eaten with many of the local people to celebrate the birthday of Wally's son-in-law, who is a true Bahamian. There were some trees offering shelter from the heat, and for a short time I sat down with a drink of fresh orange, no doubt from Florida, and relaxed watching the stars coming out ready for another Caribbean evening.

When I checked into the hotel I was met by the smiling face of Wally's daughter and her husband the hotel manager. She had just come out from the kitchen where she had been supervising the hotel suppers. They were pleased to see me and to get the latest news of Wally, as well as to receive a small box of spare parts for their car. The bits were needed to start the engine, and to extract the machine from the undergrowth and onto the dusty road (*all the roads were dusty*).

My accommodation was free being a friend of the family. I could have stayed in Wally's empty house the other end of the island, but that would have been rather lonely. It made sense to stay in the hotel by the harbour in such beautiful and tranquil surroundings. I had the added pleasure of talking to Wally's family and the local people.

After being lulled into a good night's sleep by the sound of waves rolling on the seashore, I awoke refreshed, breakfasted on fresh fruit, coffee, homemade bread and jam, and watched the sun rise in a clear deep blue sky. I spent a happy morning chatting to the islanders about nothing in particular; they are not really interested in our European problems. I must say, in such idyllic surroundings it was good not to have to think of anywhere further east than the beach.

Bearing in mind the developing clouds and bidding fond farewells I made a midday departure hoping to miss the build-up of the afternoon thunderstorms, though with a 4-hour trip that was probably not going to be possible. There was the added problem of my fuel endurance being only just sufficient – so hopefully no big detours for weather avoidance. With all that in mind I set course for the Turks and Caicos Islands.

Quite often talking on the radio is a hit and miss affair in the West Indies, due to the various accents, and the poor reception at low altitudes; so you are very much on your own. Fortunately, most bad weather can be seen when the visibility is as good as it was on this trip.

There is a Unicom common frequency of 122.80 on VHF, which is used by pilots outside main airport control. It is useful for getting updates on weather systems, and to check whether or not any of the numerous airstrips used for emergencies had been closed.

One of the airstrips in the northern Exuma group of Islands I flew over was Staniel Cay. The time before, Wally and I went visiting this little strip as he had a Cessna 206 stolen from Opa-Locka airport and he heard a rumour that the plane was on one of the islands. The Cessna 206 was a brilliant plane for drug smugglers. A large single engine aircraft with a powerful engine, big chunky tyres, a roomy cabin with seven seats or - with them removed - cargo space. It is capable of landing on short unmade airstrips; perfect for illegal haulers. Planes are often stolen, used for smuggling, then left on some airstrip when the smugglers have finished their clandestine work. Contrary to expectations the stolen planes are seldom damaged, as it is common sense to leave the plane relatively unharmed as this creates less adverse publicity for the smuggler. Insurance is a powerful media and if there were many destroyed planes, the newspapers would have a field day with all the adverse publicity that usually goes with any plane incident.

The aircraft proved to be the very machine that Wally was looking for, and soon afterwards he managed to get it back to Miami to be checked out and cleaned up. That was after the Drug Squad had given the plane a good check over and obviously before someone else came along and stole the plane again! It would eventually be sold to someone who would little suspect what had been its last cargo.

There was a Customs office at Miami airport that dealt in stolen planes. If the owner could not or did not want to be found the captured planes were sold at an auction. The problem which concerned me was that the planes would invariably not have any logbooks and this would make it extremely difficult to export out of the USA. Besides which, you can imagine the condition of the aircraft after being used for clandestine missions. The aircraft would have to be stripped and rebuilt before it could be issued with a new set of documents and release papers.

Cessna make a large range of planes, from the little C152 right up to real highflying super luxury pressurised twin-engine business jets. The little Cessna 152 was totally useless for any form of smuggling unless it was for microbes or Leprechauns! It had only two seats and the passenger seat was stacked with a life raft and an overnight bag; anything more then the plane would not get in the air. With two persons in the plane, you really had to be on good terms with each other as it was not only shoulders that rubbed together! With a combination of a small engine and high temperatures, which planes do not like, it barely lifted off the ground. It climbed a bit like Dumbo the flying elephant and had the acceleration of a turtle. The sad fact is that quite a number of light aircraft accidents are the sole result of planes constructed with underpowered engines.

Flying low over the water and looking look straight down to the sea bottom, large Manta and Sting Rays as well as the odd shark appear as large murky shadows making me shudder, and ensuring I kept more than a watchful eye on the fuel gauge. Passing numerous little islands and open sea at all of 80 miles per hour, at last, after some 310 miles from Great Exuma to Turks & Caicos, arrival at Providenciales International was imminent. I have to say that I was not certain if this was the correct island or even the correct airport. There are a lot of islands in the Turks & Caicos group including Providenciales & Caicos Cays, north Caicos, Grand Caicos, east Caicos, and south Caicos and then finally Grand Turk. Whoever named this group of islands lacked imagination, which is surprising considering the wonderful variety of names throughout the Caribbean.

How anyone could get around without becoming confused was beyond me. I am joking really but it can be a little nerve-racking at times. I was not taking the easy way out by using a Global Positioning System commonly known as the GPS. This instrument today has a database of every airport in the world along with all the approach routes, and if anything makes flying too easy! Besides which, there was a certain amount of satisfaction and enjoyment navigating the old-fashioned way with charts, pen and paper. GPS navigational systems had only just come out in the mid 1980's. Bulky and consuming a lot of power as well as costing well over a thousand pounds, they were not so accurate as those of the 21st century. Today GPS is used by nearly everyone be it in a car, plane, ship or in the pocket of a hiker roaming the countryside.

The Author standing by the Cessna 152 at Turks & Caicos Islands en route to the Dominican Republic. The main international airport on a busy day! (photo by the baggage handler).

After landing, and being made very welcome by the airport staff, I refuelled the plane ready for the morning, and moments later headed off to the nearest hotel, which was conveniently situated by the beach. The very fact that all hotels are on the beach seemed to have eluded me and anyway a sumptuous seafood dinner was awaiting a hungry pilot. Turtle was on the menu along with Conch. Normally I would not go for this type of seafood but, just for once, I tried them both and have to say that they were truly delicious. Indeed, having rarely seen them on a subsequent menu maybe there is now a protection order on these creatures.

Staying at the Turtle Cove Yacht and Tennis resort on the island of Provo within the 40 or so islands in the Turks & Caicos group was a great treat, and certainly somewhere to go back to one fine day. There are miles of golden sands and many reefs to dive on and it does not come much better than that.

Many boats of all descriptions ply their way between the islands, big and small, sailing, motor cruisers and the odd catamaran. It was a delight to see some British flagged yachts that had courageously sailed across the Atlantic Ocean. Ships of all sizes have made their way across on the south-westerly trade wind routes for hundreds of years, and though it has increased tenfold in recent times, it does not belittle the challenge and sacrifice people have to make. Whilst pilots are prepared to cross an ocean in a little plane, sailing across a large sea requires a different mentality. Seasickness affects many people, and to be bounced around on huge waves for weeks on end does not seem to me the ideal way to travel. A standard departure leaving European waters would be heading for safe havens such as the Azores, Grand Canary Islands, Madeira and mainland Portugal or even the Cape Verde Islands. The exodus would coincide with the end of the hurricane season – so around October/ November is time to set sail for the Caribbean. Depending on your departure point, it is just a few weeks to the paradise islands. The sailor needs the constitution of an elephant, and unlimited time on his hands. The big advantage is that you are effectively travelling with your home - no hotel bills. The wind is free so the costs are low in comparison to flying. So yes, my being in this part of the world is a delight, but this will all change once I'm heading to Canada and the frozen north.

Departure for the Dominican Republic in the Cessna 152 was to be a late morning affair after a swim in the warm clear waters in front of the hotel. However, the peace was soon shattered when a waiter rushed out waving his hands in the air. This very excited person explained that the airport had called reception to advise me of a heavy rainstorm building up on my route, and suggesting that I prepare for an immediate departure to avoid the forthcoming thunderstorm. I packed my bag and with the airport being so close I had the engine running and preparing for takeoff within half an hour.

The Dominican Republic strangely enough wasn't mentioned in my pilot's guidebook nor was the Republic of Haiti, being the other end of the island. So I set off not being too sure of the awaiting reception. *(The subsequent edition of the guidebook rectified the omissions)*

Two and a bit hours later having passed under some stormy clouds which had not yet unleashed their heavy load, I made my approach inbound from Providenciales airport for Customs clearance at Puerto Plata. The small semi-military airport was a little nerve racking as armed guards came out and surrounded the little Cessna 152. Everyone is so paranoid about drugs that they think that every plane regardless of size is carrying something illegal. Language can be a problem, in some countries the soldiers are quite often poorly trained and not too well educated. However, a little smile and a wave of the British Passport seemed to make things easier. You might think that wearing a pilot uniform in a tiny 2-seater machine is maybe a little over the top, but in these places you would be arrested if you were dressed like a civilian and were wandering around an airport in the `wrong` areas.

I will not start raving on about security, but even in European airports including some very major ones, it is amazing where you can go when looking the part. In 18 years of part-time flying, I can count on two hands the times when Security wanted to see my licence and insurance; although my pilot's photographic ID card had to be worn at all times. This has changed completely with the onset of the dark hand of terrorism, and Security has gone totally the other way. I was the person many years ago who the Customs always used to stop when coming back to England in a car from France before the end of the duty free wine era. They would for some reason assume by my guilty look that I was carrying more than my wine allowance, *(unfortunately they were usually right)* so I would be stopped virtually every time – hence my becoming a teetotaller.*(Joke)*.

When the airport guards at Puerto Plata realised that I was British, and upon my opening the little plane door for them to see inside *(just in case they thought there was something hidden)* they took on a more friendly approach. I also showed them a little bit of respect, which can go a long way with nervous guards, and shaking hands can form a temporary bond.

A large passenger jet had just come in from Quebec full of, naturally enough, Quebecians, *(French Canadians)*. Quite a coincidence as I would hopefully be going there in a few days time. Some of the more nervous elderly passengers started talking to me in French, which fortunately I could understand, having learnt French many years ago as a student. They were concerned about soldiers with guns, and not being able to speak Spanish the Canadians were a little in the `oh dear why did we come here` mood. My Spanish was very basic so apart from possibly ordering 380 coffees with milk for the arrivals, I was not really able to help. However as a friendly person with the assurance an airman's uniform gave, I did lend a hand until the Courier arrived and took the holidaymakers to the Customs and normality. Indeed, tourism plays such an important part in producing income for the islands that they have to lay off the heavy-handed approach.

I feel that Airlines & tour operators do not always understand the problems that one can come across in the smaller regional airports. It can be quite disconcerting for inexperienced passengers to descend from the security of the plane and be suddenly confronted by language and temperature differences. They initially see quite a different perspective from their home airport - many of the tourist spots in the developing world during the 80`s had by our standards quite basic airport facilities. The effect of modern airline transport is to propel one rapidly, in relative comfort, (*complete with onboard entertainment, food and drink*) from your home to, within a few hours, a totally different and - dare I say it – possibly an intimidating and dangerous environment. There seems to be an air of mistrust that predominates at airports, or am I being paranoid?

Departing from Puerto Plata in the Cessna, a couple of hour's flight brought me to the capital, Santa

Domingo, my final destination some 120 miles the other side of the island. Part of the flight had taken me over an area called Jamao Al Norte. This can be only described as a mass of small green extremely pointed hills similar to the shape of egg cartons. Perhaps it was created from some long ago volcanic disturbance, or by a very large prehistoric chicken laying eggs!

With excellent visibility and with the odd cloud offering some shade from the oppressive heat the flight was easy. Heading south-by-south-east I passed the halfway mark of Bonao town with mountain peaks topping 9,000 feet behind the remote settlement. No snow to ski down the slope into a beachside bar in this tropical paradise. On the other side of the mountain range lay Haiti a country in political turmoil *(not recommended as an alternative)*. Crossing the main railway line in the foothills of the border, I turned away from the mountains. I followed the southern railway line into Santa Domingo keeping well clear of the main airport, De Las Americas International. From San Cristobal at the southern-most tip it was a straight-in approach to the old international airport which is now only for small business planes. Centred in the heart of the shantytown area, with houses right up to the perimeter fence, you virtually touch the roofs to land the plane, and the thought of an engine failing there does not bear thinking about.

The Caribbean is a very diverse area with numerous different languages, cultures and nationalities. One could almost liken it to Central Europe but on a smaller scale, with water instead of motorways between the countries. As with Europe, there are very poor and very well off areas and it is a matter of luck into which island you are born. It is funny to think that 250 miles further east is the island of Puerto Rico *(American)* and a further 130 or so miles east brings you to Anguilla *(United Kingdom)*. The southern island Saint Martin some 14 miles south is French; 120 miles west is Haiti and 220 miles north are the Caicos Islands *(United Kingdom)*. The Caribbean is truly international within relatively short distances. There are many more islands close by, but I would need to consult an atlas to catalogue them.

I left the little Cessna 152 with the local flying school; which comprised of a corrugated shed with basic table and chairs - no hi tech computer gear at all. I went to stay the night with Jose´ the flying club's instructor. Living in a small pleasant house in a downtown estate, we spent an agreeable early evening meeting neighbours and sitting on the garden wall chatting to people who had never been off the island. They all had a great deal of respect for our royal family and were very interested in hearing about London and our way of life. Suddenly half way through our chatting everything went dark; it was a *`brown out`* *as opposed to a `black out`*. It was evidently quite common for the power to suddenly conk out and leave everyone in the gloom. Nobody seemed perturbed, and within a few minutes lighted candles appeared everywhere; it seemed that people carried them around so they were always prepared. Some while later power was restored as if nothing had happened, except perhaps for a subsequent increase in the birth rate! Later on that evening I went out with Jose´ to an open-air nightclub, which went well - perhaps a little too well. Great music blaring out and people dancing; with the stars as the Club's ceiling. The Bacardi and coke served by the busy waiters were rather excessive on the Bacardi. Local rum being cheaper to produce than coke, it was three-quarters rum topped up with ice-cold coke and fresh sliced lime. The people were very friendly to an Englishman who became somewhat inebriated!

After turning down a job flying at the local Club, I made my way to bed. The mosquitoes were not so friendly and waking up in the morning to a mass of lumps, I realised that I had forgotten to unfurl my mosquito net. There must have been a few drunken mosquitoes that day! I had a monumental hangover, but no chance of a lie-in as I needed to catch the midday flight back to Miami. Oh well, at least someone else is flying me back. Leaving Jose´ and his mother who kindly looked after me for the overnight stay and feeling envious of them living in such a beautiful island, I said my fond farewells, and jumped in the taxi for the ride to the Airport.

My departure out of the Dominican Republic was in a 40 year old Boeing 707. Boarding the plane at De Las

Americas International Airport, I sat back and relaxed into a trance of nostalgic history. Though these planes had stopped flying with the major airlines 20 to 25 years before, it appears that there were no shortage of takers and many of the poorer countries still fly the lovely old Boeings from the late 1960`s.

Wally kindly met me at Miami International Airport, and propelled me home in his luxurious Lincoln limo. During the drive, he mentioned a job vacancy, co-pilot flying a DC3 with a similar age to the Boeing 707 I had just flown in as a passenger. Based at Opa-Locka airport transporting cargo around the Caribbean sounded really great. The pay was not as good as UK rates but I would have accepted without hesitation, for the whole area is a flyers paradise. However, having commitments back in the UK, it was with great reluctance that I had to decline. Later Wally let me get in the old beast so I could see what I would be missing. Somehow, it was reminiscent of Denis's Cessna 336, except an awful lot bigger, and complete with torn seats and oil leaks.

An Extremely Short Hop

Back in Opa-Locka, Denis's plane was about ready for a flight test. We gingerly mounted it and had to taxi for 10 minutes before reaching the take off area. Turning and lining up on the centre line, we were cleared for take-off with what seemed like miles of runway in front of us; that was a good thing, bearing in mind that this was the first flight the 336 had made for many years. On the take-off run keeping an eye on the rear engine gauges to ensure that the embarrassment of attempting to take off with one engine did not happen to us, we staggered into the air. Mind you, with such a long runway and lightly loaded, no doubt the plane could have made it into the blue yonder on one engine. However, it became apparent that we were not climbing very fast and looking out of the window we noticed the flaps, which are normally deployed for landing, were slowly coming down out of their recesses. Checking the flap switches and muttering a few comments did nothing to alleviate the problem. The main thing was that we were climbing, albeit slowly.

Thank goodness the flaps decided to stop at the first level otherwise it would have been nigh on impossible to have continued any sort of test flight. Pulling out the circuit breakers did not help as power was required to retract as well as deploy. Cessna make powerful flaps commonly known as `barn doors` and the full stage of flaps is only used when in the final throws of landing with no wind and on a very short runway.

Upon reaching a couple of thousand feet and levelling off, I noticed what appeared to be water running out of the back of the wings. This was mighty strange as it was a red-hot summer's day with no clouds whatsoever. Making a hasty retreat for the ground *(via the runway)*, we stopped outside the maintenance workshop. The `smoking mechanic` who for a change was not actually smoking came out and suggested that the `water` was fuel, leaking probably because the seals had given up sealing many years ago; on top of which the flap motor switch was faulty.

It makes me laugh, derisively, when after risking life and limb in the air, the person on the ground comes out with such a statement, and in a tone of voice implying that is what was going to happen anyway. Considering that we had some 4,600 miles to go in a few days time, it was even more concerning. Denis by this stage was running out of patience, seriously troubled whether his beloved plane would ever be ready, he was beginning to seethe like a pressure cooker about to blow. I moved discreetly to one side whilst he made appropriate comments to the aircraft engineer.

We called in Wally Evans who then suggested taking the plane to the main Cessna agent on the field to complete the work. This was embarrassing - there is this super smart hangar with posh jets, and we turn up towed by one of those little tractors. However, I give them fair credit, no silly remarks were made and they assured us given a few weeks, and a lot of dollars, the 336 would be ready. The pilot facilities were a vast improvement to the bucket in the corner of the hangar in the previous place! TV, coffee, free donuts and glossy magazines which, upon reading, opened a window on how the very rich and famous live in that part of the world.

Whilst walking around the numerous businesses, I noticed that a Piper Warrior languishing in a corner had a `for sale` notice stuck on the window. Next door to an engineer's workshop there was a small flying school where occasionally we used to have a coffee and a chat. The Club's owner said that the Piper Warrior was for sale as things were a little quiet and he wanted to get rid of a surplus plane. The Warrior sort of beckoned me to come closer. It seemed to appear happy to see someone take an interest - if a plane can give that impression!

I had already made tentative arrangements with my bank in the UK, as I was looking for a plane for a client. I had promised that if the right one came along I would purchase subject to a survey. The Piper Warrior has a single 150 hp engine, which pulls the plane along at the rate of 110 miles an hour, and seemed just right. Seating four people with a small amount of luggage or two to three depending on the weight of the baggage, it is a good little plane, easy to fly and with no hidden vices, perfect for local flying. It is probably one of the most popular light aircraft, along with the Cessna 172. The Club said it was available at a very fair price. Ok I know that I am a sucker and thought, well, we have to get back home and Denis's plane will not be ready for another 4 or 5 weeks, so might as well fly this one back to England.

I spoke to my private pilot client in the UK and he was very happy to go ahead with the deal. As he said on the phone, if it makes the trip in one piece it will prove the reliability and condition of the plane!

The purchase was simple enough and with the issue of an export Certificate of Airworthiness, the plane was mine within a few days. Unfortunately some American States, including Florida, have a sales tax levy. This meant my going to an official government office the other side of Florida in order to obtain an exemption, as the plane would be leaving the USA.

Then a slight hiccup – I had recently flown back a twin-engine plane which had existing long range fuel tanks *(with a fair tail wind,)* and I realised there was no way the little Warrior was going to make it; even flying the so-called northern corridor via Greenland. The Warrior's small engine and poor carrying capacity meant that any route was out without adding extra fuel capacity. Working with another maintenance organisation, having little faith in the motley crew that had been originally working on Denis's plane, I decided to get a 50-gallon ferry tank fitted in Opa-Locka. Rather there than Monckton, Canada, just in case there was a possibility of flying the southern route from South America/Caribbean to West Africa. I arranged for the rear seats to be removed to give the floor space required and placed the seats squashed flat in a void behind.

One of the navigational problems crossing an ocean or a large land mass is on making a `great circle route`; which is the shortest distance between two places on the earth's surface. It is along the arc of the circle whose mathematical plane passes through the centre of the earth. That is why for example all airlines, including Virgin Atlantic, British Airways, American Airlines etc. fly the particular route they do in order to arrive at their destination.

The Piper Warrior in sunny Florida waiting for a buyer. The Old Grumman seaplane just behind would have suited us better for the trip we were undertaking (photo by author).

99

From some mid position over Greenland the North Pole was nearer than London. Wrong way, no more time for dreaming, I must concentrate. Back to mapping the course -   firstly one gets hold of a Gnomonic chart covering the required area; which is effectively part of the globe flattened onto a sheet of paper with the meridians of longitude splayed out like a fan, and the parallels of latitude curved. The more normal chart/map that is used is the Mercator chart with its rectangular grids of latitude and longitude lines. However if you used this type of chart for long journeys of say one thousand miles or more, the line drawn on the chart *(called a rhumb line)* would not be the actual route flown or sailed; with the consequence of missing an all-important island for refuelling, or flying into something rather hard! So you plot the course on a Gnomonic chart and then transfer a series of latitude and longitude points from the great circle route and plot them to the Mercator chart. You then join up the lines, which are in fact short rhumb lines which then form the curve, and that is basically all there is to creating a circle route!

An important point if one is contemplating flying towards the higher Latitudes *(Arctic or Antarctic)*, is the use of the great circle route. Lines of longitude converge to a point at the poles, and the rhumb line effectively becomes redundant. Every heading is a great circle regardless of the distance involved. The successful explorers who have reached the poles would have the satisfaction of running around the world in a few seconds!

Nowadays it is as well to realise that electronics including the GPS can go wrong, so it is important not to rely solely on technology. I always like to have a chart course backed up by old-fashioned navigation at the ready.

Looking at a map, Bermuda, the West Indies, Madeira, The Azores, and Canaries are not in a sensible order for re-fuelling and most importantly, the trade winds that have blown for centuries bringing over the sailing boats from Europe are westerly in direction. Little planes do not fly very fast and a headwind of say 25 miles an hour, which is nothing, can add 20% onto the fuel needed.

The Jet Stream would be very useful in the northern latitudes and indeed all the `schedules` save some 12% or even 18% by catching a ride on this fast moving easterly stream of air. However, it means flying approximately at 38,000 feet and as we would be bumping along at 8,000 feet we would not be able to take advantage of that! I therefore decided that whilst the southern route in some ways was more hospitable from a weather point of view, it needed too great a fuel range. There was another slight problem, Denis had decided to hitch a lift with me rather than fly in luxury with Virgin Atlantic. Although he had a stack of work awaiting him in the UK, I suspect the real reason he chose to fly back with me was his sense of adventure. Relaxing on a commercial flight, or flying a single engine plane – no contest! This meant that there was precious little room in the plane for the two of us plus luggage, bearing in mind that the back of the plane would already be full with a 50-gallon fuel drum and the two squashed rear seats. In the end we managed to squeeze everything in and still be only 10% overloaded. The overload was permitted on a Ferry Flight, but with a drum of fuel behind us, this made the plane a type of flying bomb with us in front ready to be blasted into eternity. Not the best way to travel, but immensely preferable to going down into the cold and rough waters of the Atlantic because of lack of fuel. Besides which, I needed all the luck in the world flying a 15-year-old plane back on one engine without worrying about fuel. The airspeed was also degraded with the load and I only managed to get around 100 miles an hour instead of the more normal 115 mph.

A High Frequency Radio Transmitter was also required, as the normal VHF radio fitted to planes would not have the range. They teach you when doing the radio licence that different frequencies work better depending on the time of day and varying with your geographical location. It was most certainly a more complicated piece of equipment than most radios. Atmospherics also play a big part - HF radios crackle, hiss and fade, more in keeping with the old valve radios I used to play with in my teens. So I felt quite at home and readily accepted that there was no way we could talk to anyone with the `Mickey Mouse` temporary installation on the little plane. A 40-foot aerial had to be installed on the Warrior - not a problem to the large airliners whose length can accommodate such a `washing line` from the cockpit roof to the tip of the fin. Today, of course, HF radio can be linked via satellite. However, it is a problem with small planes *(who seldom need such a radio)* and the only way was to have a type of fishing reel fitted inside the cockpit with a little hole beneath and a heavy weight on the bottom of the line. The aerial installation could be done at Monckton on the Canadian border where in any case we had to `check out` with the Authorities.

On the last twin I flew back the aerial was indeed as per the airliners, extending from cockpit to fin – but it did not work very well. The idea of a fishing line was that, when at altitude, one can unwind the copper cable and lengthen the aerial making reception clearer, or at least that was the idea. After various attempts to talk to someone without much success, the line was wound back into the cockpit. It was rather important to remember not to leave the long line dangling when landing, as 40 foot of wire could do some damage to the plane not to mention what a large lead weight might end up doing to anyone in the vicinity!.

Thinking about all that water to cross reminded me of my ditching drill which I did many years ago in

Portsmouth. A very good friend of mine, Angus, was the chief experimental dive officer. He was a civilian naval commander attached to the Royal Navy underwater diving unit, and taught the use of the metallic bronze diving helmet *(hard hat)* suit and the more flexible scuba diving equipment. Holding the world record for the deepest dive of 2,020 feet with an experimental hard hat immersion suit, and looking like something out of the Jules Verne novel 20,000 Leagues Under The Sea, I doubt very much if there was anyone better qualified as a teacher. The training was unique inasmuch as the water tank, 65-foot deep, was perched on top of a building!

This was remarkable; there you were 50 feet or so below the surface, looking out at a panoramic view of the Solent through portholes conveniently put in the side of the tank. I am sure that the people on the ferryboats and pleasure craft bobbing around the sea would have been quite amazed to know that they were being watched by a diver under the water but above their heads! It was even possible to see the navy planes landing at Lee-on-Solent (*since closed*), and the Islander aircraft landing at Bembridge, Isle of Wight.

The training and jumping out of the rotating platform simulating a plane or helicopter entering water, was not much fun as it was so easy to get vertigo and become extremely giddy and confused. Happily, there were willing hands waiting in the water just in case help was needed. Only when you simulate an incident can you begin to realise just how hard, and perhaps how virtually impossible it is to actually survive for real.

The water tank in Portsmouth near the harbour with the rotating and spinning capsule that simulated a plane ditching in the sea. You can see daylight through the portholes and the view over the famous Solent. Noticeable is how calm is the water in the tank, a bit of a shock to the system if one has to abandon ones flying machine in an ocean with 20 foot high waves and blowing a gale. The black thing at the end of the fuselage lifted the helicopter/plane cabin above the water. It was a computerised nightmare that mimicked the real thing (photo by author).

However, training is a very important part of any syllabus when man or woman meets a different environment, and it was something I took extremely seriously. You never know when a malevolent fate would play its hand – usually at a most inconvenient time. Hopefully, if I had to ditch a plane there would be someone ready to help.

A mile further south of Bembridge is the small grass landing strip of Sandown Airport, very popular with private pilots, possibly because of a very friendly run tearoom! Problem with the grass strip at Sandown is that great care is needed during heavy downpours. Planes with the more delicate retractable landing gear are prone to damage, making Bembridge's hard runway a better choice. The airfield at Bembridge goes back to the Schneider Cup Trophy before the 1st World war. In more recent years the famous twin engine and three engine Brittan Norman Islander and Tri-lander aircraft were built there. These were tough planes for island hopping, and desert locations, and were even fitted with skis for snowy and cold climates. Getting around most of the islands surrounding the UK or in the Pacific Ocean, you will invariably be flown in an Islander.

The Schneider Trophy that put the Solent area on the map was a race to prove that a seaplane could fly as fast as a normal aeroplane. Substantial money prizes were offered in 1913 by Jacques Schneider, a French aviation enthusiast, when the first race for the trophy was held at Monaco. This race was won by the famous French pilot, Prevost, who was flying a Deperdussin monoplane. Thought I knew planes, but that was a new one on me.

From Portsmouth across the narrow access to the Solent, these planes would come roaring past at very low altitude much to the excitement of the cheering crowds. The Supermarine was to become R. J. Mitchell's famous Spitfire that did so well in protecting the homelands against the enemy during the conflict 1939 to 1945.

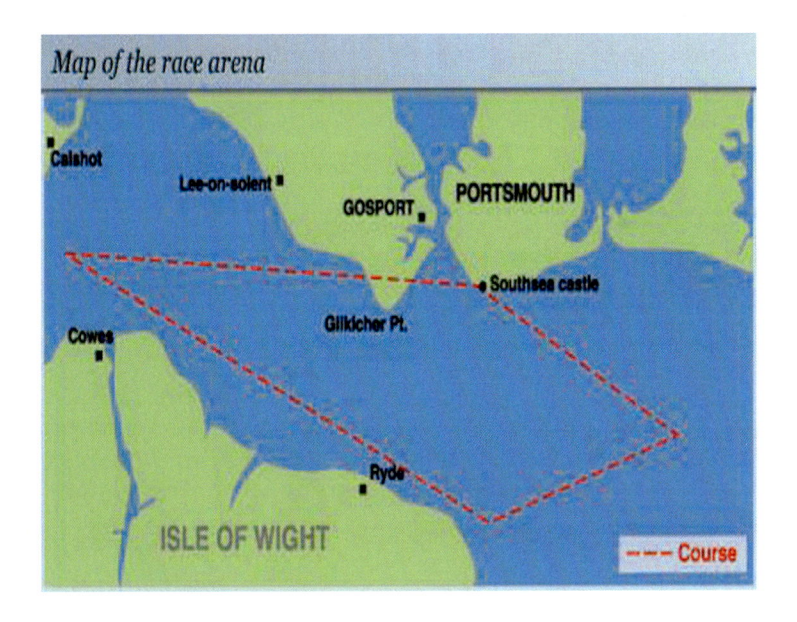

Map of the race arena

Owing to the 1st World War no further races were held until 1919, when after an English pilot having won the race in 1914 at Monaco, the Schneider Cup Race was brought to Bournemouth. Various locations were used in the ensuing years until in 1929 it was staged in Bembridge. The participation was restricted to several aircraft including two Supermarines built by Mitchell, and the S.6s flown by Commander Waghorn (*see picture*) and Commander Atcherley, and the modified D'Arcy Creig's Supermarine S.5. Hundreds of thousands of spectators, mainly at Portsmouth & Southsea beach, attended the final race in magnificent weather. Waghorn whose name describes this charismatic pilot won the race at speeds up to 500 kilometres (300mph). A tremendous achievement and a big boost for the morale of Great Britain. The majority of people watching would have difficulty in grasping such swiftness as the main transport then was the horse and cart.

A story is told of Mitchell's reaction to the win. As he got off the launch and walked up Calshot slipway an aircraft engineer stepped forward saying, "congratulations, I am pleased that you have won for your sake", Mitchell replied, "it is not for my sake, but for our country's". Prophetic words considering what was going to happen a few years later in 1939!

Fortunately in 2006 I happened to be on a boat in Bembridge harbour whilst this event was taking place, and I had to smile to myself because I could not help but notice that the 337 participating in the race was still just as noisy as the 336. Denis would have been amazed and probably proud to see the luxury version of his beloved plane flying in style.

An Anniversary of the Schneider Trophy September 2006 over flying Bembridge Airport. The incredible thing is the lower plane - the Cessna 337 the retractable (unpressurised) version of Denis's old Cessna 336,! (File photo).

There are many aircraft races held in the 21st century, but nothing can ever match the classic days of the early flying years. The Americans still hold various air competitions; the most famous being the `round the pylon race` - low level and with highly modified engines and airframes it still is one of the most dangerous competitive sports. Perhaps that is why pilots wear wings as badges, and perchance their belief in their guardian angel!

I often think there must have been a guardian angel taking care of me, because I was indeed fortunate to come out with my life intact after some of the scrapes I got into. My pot-holing and scuba diving days had their moments, but I survived thanks to our training and the comradeship of friends who are still with me today. Even my sailing days of crossing the English Channel at night had their fill of excitement.

There is the good old saying, *'there are bold pilots and old pilots but no bold old pilots`* which tends to be true. If you take a look at the pilots in the airports flying airliners, amongst the new young recruits you will see older men, with greying hair and greying beards, experienced men who have 30 or more years of flying knowledge behind them– they are the pilots who take care of you – a smile and a thank you as you leave the plane is always appreciated. They do care!

The uninformed say that pilots are just bus drivers in the sky, and to those people I would suggest they spend a little time studying the flight manuals, and perhaps realising the intense training required, and the many years pilots spend learning Meteorology and Aviation Law. Then, people might understand how difficult it really is! Pilots need to have the ability to make snap life saving decisions, such as in early 2009 in the USA, when the pilots of a large passenger jet made an emergency landing in the Hudson river with no fatalities. Most pilots have to find many thousands of pounds *(at least £30,000)* in order to undertake the basic commercial training. The majority would have spent several years flying little planes as an instructor, or doing charter work, to build the hours needed for the transition from small to large planes. Then they have to achieve the various type ratings needed for each different aircraft. Being a pilot is a labour of love; it is either in your genes or not. Pilots have to take out a very comprehensive medical insurance, the health criteria is very high, lose your medical and that is your flying career out of the window. I had a medical problem in 2002 and was grounded for a while. A year after the tragic and cowardly attack on America, September 2001, forever known as 9/11 when the world changed.

A Goodbye To Sunny Florida Hop

A long way from Bembridge and the Isle of Wight, we were at last sitting in the Piper Warrior at the holding point to the runway in Opa-Locka Airport. I finished the cockpit paperwork and called on the radio that I was ready for departure to New York. With one 150 hp engine running up front *(the only one),* we took off with a very heavy load and heavy hearts, heading north leaving behind Miami and the warmth of Florida. Air Traffic Control wished us well and we were cleared to our assigned altitude of 9,000 feet. With a high temperature outside and our overloaded little plane, it was a slow climb at around 70 miles an hour and a rate of just 400 decreasing to 300 feet a minute. Think of us next time when you are in a large multi-engine jet airliner thundering through the air climbing at 5,000 + feet a minute.

It was good to have Denis with me as flying on your own can be lonely and, besides, we always seemed to have so much to talk about. By the time we had finished all our checks, had a nibble of our in-flight meal – a sandwich *(one day I will look like one the amount I have eaten)* - we levelled off at the assigned altitude and headed to the colder regions.

The weather conditions with nothing but blue sky for miles around were comforting, though in our cramped seats in the Warrior we could hardly relax, but we did appreciate the marvellous views. I thought about Brian, the ferry pilot whose job it would be to take to the UK the good old Cessna 336. He had more time to spare than we did and he needed it; we learned later that he broke down twice on the journey back!

The fuel tank that was taking up the rear seat in the Warrior was being used first in order to check that the pump transfer system was working correctly prior to our flight across the Arctic Ocean. Fuel vapour is extremely dangerous and explosive, and whilst the tank was being used, it was very important to keep an eye on the external venting arrangement. Even when empty this potential time bomb needed careful monitoring.

Going up towards the Eastern Seaboard brought back memories of one of my previous ferry flights some 2 years prior, when flying a twin engine Piper Seneca along this route. Heading from Sarasota Airport, Bradenton, Florida towards North Carolina, I started to feel really sick and breathless. My fingers were turning blue and there I was at 12,500 feet, flying on my own, wondering what was happening. Unbeknown to me a fuel pipe had ruptured leaking fuel into the cockpit. Although the plane had built-in oxygen, it had been disconnected for that ferry flight due to certification problems (*allowed to work in the States but needed modifying for UK airspace – what a crazy world*). In fact, if I had had oxygen, I would have been able to carry on as the mask fitted over the nose and mouth, blocking out the air in the cockpit. This paradoxically could have made the position worse as I might not have realised how serious the situation was becoming. I made a *'May Day'* distress call to Raleigh Durham International North Carolina which was some 60 miles ahead and informed them of my problem. They immediately cleared me for an emergency landing and told me to concentrate on flying; they would give compass headings to the airport and even tell me what height I should maintain. This was very important as I was having real problems in concentrating. From my present altitude and distance, it would take approximately 20 minutes to the airport.

Although there were airports nearer it somehow seemed logical to continue to my original destination, besides which, wherever I ended up, it would take around 8 - 12 minutes to get to the approach altitude. Emergency rapid descents were not advisable in my current circumstance. Things were getting worse in the cockpit and I could not breathe properly, so I rolled the airways route chart on my lap into a tube and put one end in my mouth and the other sticking out of a very small flap in the cockpit side window. This helped me to breathe in clean albeit cold fresh air, but made havoc with talking on the radio in the approach stages, though it certainly did help me to keep going. Telling Control that I was not sure if I could make it to the airport, but there was a large lake ahead *(coincidently near to where a friend of mine lives with his family)* and maybe I could land on the water to keep clear of any people. Not being a seaplane this was a daft idea, but my brain was not functioning correctly. My eyes were watering badly and it was getting difficult to read the instruments. I wanted to be sick, but fortunately that did not happen. Control encouraged me to keep flying, as it was only another 10 minutes or so to the airport. They even offered to send up a `shepherd` aircraft to guide me in if I could not concentrate anymore. Thankfully, this offer was not needed, it was just staying conscious that was my primary concern.

The fire crew who were watching *(no doubt from a safe position)* told me afterwards that my flying was like the pendulum of a clock swinging side to side. That may not say very much about my flying but I did have a genuine excuse. With Air Traffic Control giving me instructions all the way down and putting the schedule planes in holding patterns out of harm's way, I lowered the landing gear and miraculously landed the plane without any damage to anything. It goes to show how well planes are designed that with little input they land without any harm. Mind you, the runway was two and a half miles long so no problem. Had the weather been bad then it is highly unlikely that I would have survived. With no co-pilot and being so ill, flying on instruments would not have been possible. Once again, my guardian angel had come to the rescue.

Automatically, even with a fuzzy brain, I shut down the engines on the runway, and just managed to open the door to the scream of fire engine sirens and the ambulance. I seem to remember being gently helped out of the plane by the fire crew and being placed on a stretcher and then I recall very little until waking up in the casualty department of Raleigh hospital.

After some tests and an overnight stay I was pronounced fit, albeit very tired, and discharged. It had been discovered that the fuel line had burst in the starboard wing and a venturi effect had drawn fuel vapour into the cockpit of the plane. I had been effectively breathing in neat fuel fumes. The Fire

Chief was amazed that the plane had not blown up, for any little spark when operating one of the numerous buttons and switches in the cockpit could have set off the explosive fuel vapour. Those were the days when I smoked, and I shuddered to think what would have happened if I had `lit up` a cigarette! There would have been one massive explosion, and little bits of me and the plane would have fallen over North Carolina like used confetti. I never touched a cigarette again!

Because I had come up from Florida, and the cause of my temporary disability had not been completely assessed, the local FBI decided that I might have been high on drugs. They wanted to search my plane and asked if I had any objections. With several plain clothed heavily armed officers all around me, a rather timid, `no - help yourself` was the reply! Obviously, there were no drugs and after checking my credentials, the FBI departed on their merry way, and the sheriff of the local county police offered his help if needed, which was very decent of him. I had to leave the plane at Raleigh as it was impounded whilst the FAA *(Federal Aviation Administration)* and the CAA *(Civil Aviation Authority)* were notified. Even the British Embassy was involved in sorting out the bi-nation incident.

A much later Piper Seneca III, the one I flew around Europe for many years, shown here at the John Lennon Int. Airport, Liverpool where I was a frequent visitor. The pipe that ruptured on the older model was around 4 inches (100mm) on the outside of the engine narcel starboard side. (photo by author).

After due investigation it was found that the maintenance company in Florida which issued the flight certificate had not done a pressure check on the fuel lines, where this split in the pipe would have shown up. The actual cause of the split was due to the plane being left out in the sun for a very long time in south Florida without fuel, thus causing the rubber pipe connection to go brittle. It gets very hot down there and this particular model had a short rubber hose joining two fuel tanks in each wing. This hose was only in place for about a year before the design was modified and changed. What a pity I had unknowingly chosen the wrong year's model.

Meanwhile I had to submit to all the commotion and the form filling arising from the incident. A professional British pilot flying an American registered plane making an emergency landing at an International Airport caused no end of paperwork. I needed to get back to England whilst the repairs were being carried out so I bought a round ticket and in no time at all an American Airlines Boeing 777 deposited me in the UK to await the outcome of the repairs and investigation. It was a few weeks before I was able to return and complete the delivery of the plane.

Continuing with the flight in the Warrior, flying past Raleigh Durham and leaving behind memories of that nightmare in the Seneca, our journey carried on up the Eastern Seaboard heading towards New York. Passing over Kitty Hawk, North Carolina, my mind drifted back to the turn of the century, recalling that it was here that the Wright Brothers made the world's first flight in 1903 a mere 85 years ago.

They only travelled a few hundred feet on that first flight. Time and time again they tried to get their design perfect, but it was no easy task. Wilbur and Orville were intensely religious and always smartly dressed with collar and tie. They worked together making and mending bicycles until they decided to make a flying machine after reading about the idea in a newspaper. Bearing in mind that they could only fly on a near perfect day with a moderate wind, even if the weather was good on a Sunday they would not work on that day. This definitely retarded their initial progress.

*This unique picture is over 100 years old and is quite comical with Wilbur in a prone position in the damaged machine of an unsuccessful trial on December 14, 1903 at Kitty Hawk. It appears that he has his elbows on the wing, the palm of his hands supporting his chin and is contemplating the grains of sand beneath him! Either that or in a dreamy moment of humour, is he really thinking that he is flying and the grains look like people? Perhaps in a moment of panic shouting `wait a minute they **are** people! (Photo courtesy Wrights Bros Archives).*

They were reluctant and even obstinate in demonstrating the `flyer` *(a rather obvious name of for plane)* to potential customers; this actually gave a leading edge to their competitors who were clamouring for a piece of the action.

It is interesting to recall that in 1908 in the UK, near Farnborough Airport in Hampshire (*a few miles from my base Fairoaks*), a rather famous American pioneer by the name of Samuel Franklin Cody flew a biplane all of 1,400 feet at an altitude of 30 to 40 feet above a very large flat field; exceeding the Wright Brothers historic flight. In fact Cody along with fellow pioneers, including, John Dunne, Sir George Caley, and Geoffrey de Havilland, made Farnborough a hive of activity. The airport became instrumental in the development and testing of aircraft and this has continued to the present day. It is now a major regional & international business airport with some 25,000 movements a year; which just goes to show the growth rate in one hundred years.

1908 was a significant year in the development of planes and flying; everything started to take off *(sorry about the corny humour).* In less than 5 years from the start of man's first flight, there were flying machines being made and flown all over the world. In another 6 years with the onset of World War One, planes were developed into powerful semi aerobatic fairly reliable fighter aeroplanes.

The Wright brothers who pretty much started the ball rolling were slowly being left behind. They continued to make more planes and further improvements, but too late as every man and his dog were now forging ahead with the race to the skies.

With the Wright Brothers flight site over the sand dunes passing beneath us, there we were in another little plane intending to travel several thousand miles! As the plane was not pressurised I could only go to a maximum altitude of 12,000 feet without oxygen which was not normally fitted in small planes. This was immaterial anyway as the plane could not climb above that, especially with high outside temperatures.

Ensuring all was correct with the Warrior and my navigation, my mind slipped back again into the past, and I started thinking about another aircraft, `The Spirit of St. Louis` and the intrepid pilot Charles Lindbergh. Working as a mail pilot the previous year he heard of the $25,000 prize for the first flight between New York and Paris. Backed by some St. Louis businessmen Lindbergh supervised the building of his special plane and set out to win the prize.

Other teams were attempting the feat, and quite a few had met disaster. Preparing for the epic flight Lindbergh equipped himself with four sandwiches *(something I had in common with Charles Lindbergh was sandwiches!)*, two canteens of water and 451 gallons of petrol. It was May 20 1927 when he took off to make the first Transatlantic Ocean flight from New York to Paris. He `gunned` the engine of the `Spirit of St Louis` and aimed her down the dirt runway of Roosevelt Field, Long Island. Heavily laden with fuel, the plane bounced down the muddy field, gradually became airborne and barely cleared the telephone wires at the field's edge. The crowd of 500 thought they had witnessed a miracle.

Midway through the flight ice began to cling to the plane. That would have worried him a great deal, and he must have debated whether to keep on flying or go back, but he obviously decided to continue. Thirty-three and a half hours and 3,500 miles later, Charles Lindbergh crossed the coast of France, followed the River Seine to Paris and touched down at Le Bourget Field at 10:22 pm, the first person to fly the Atlantic alone.

Many of the waiting crowd of 100,000 rushed to the plane whilst it was still taxiing, and to avert the danger of people getting caught by the propeller, Lindbergh quickly switched off the engine.

Strange when you think that dozens of planes now make this trip every day without a moments thought by the thousands of passengers. Becoming an instant hero, Lindbergh was given the title, `The Lone Eagle`. His flight was a miracle, bearing in mind how unreliable the planes and engines were in those pioneering days. The plane did not have a conventional cockpit and he had to use a periscope to see out of the front. I was really glad that my little Warrior did not have such an arrangement, as it is good to see where you are going, especially as there are more things to hit in today's crowded skies.

The Spirit of St. Louis
If you look at the wing, it just seems to be bolted onto the fuselage. Just think that in the tiny claustrophobic cabin squashed underneath, CL would have spent those long hours looking out through the periscope seeking the land so far away. A very brave man. (Photo courtesy of the Lindbergh archives).

With regard to the icing that he picked up on his way over the Atlantic, this could have been the end of the flight, as because of this many planes simply disappeared without trace. De-icing systems on planes did not exist; in fact nobody really comprehended the significance of plane icing. There were numerous fatal accidents, the cause of which were not fully understood. When a plane locked in an iced up environment fell out of the sky, by the time the examiners of the wreckage made their diagnosis, the ice would have melted away leaving the investigators totally stumped as to the cause. Weather related accidents abounded for a great many years with a large loss of life. There was a time when people were turning away from flying and actually looking back to the old-fashioned ways of travel. Fortunately, over the next few decades, weather systems were meticulously studied and recorded; and radar development was underway. The Air Traffic Controllers started giving out accurate weather reports, and conditions generally improved for the aviation community.

Upon Charles Lindbergh's return to New York by passenger ship, the City gave him the largest ticker tape parade ever and President Calvin Coolidge awarded him the Distinguished Flying Cross. His feat electrified the nation and inspired enthusiastic interest in aviation. A terrible tragedy fell on the family in 1932 when his young son was kidnapped and brutally murdered. The family moved to England for several years to escape the media pressures *(some things never change),* but sadly the great man never completely recovered from the awful trauma of the loss of his son. Perhaps a sharp reminder to us all that fame can so often bring grief. Interesting to note that quite a few pioneering pilots had more than their share of personal problems. One of the downsides of being famous. Certainly Charles Lindbergh was no ordinary man; he was a tremendous leader and very charismatic. He set the world ablaze with his flights and improvements to aviation. In 1936, prior to the 2nd world war he was in Germany and was one of the few non Germans who flew German Fighters (S*ome say as a spy for the American Government).* Both he and his wife were special guests of Field Marshal Hermann Goering, the head of the German military air force, the *Luftwaffe.* Lindbergh toured German aircraft factories and was awarded the Service Cross of the German Eagle for his contributions to aviation.

The family were even toying with the thought of living there, but when the war broke out he dropped all ideas of moving to Germany and settled back in America. A wise move - it could have had bad consequences for the Americans joining the war if their top hero was living in that country. There would have been a huge outcry from the public.

Ever onwards in the Piper Warrior we left North Carolina heading towards Newark, New York. We were leaving the beautiful weather behind us and going towards the forecasted bad weather and so a hop closer to home. I could not help thinking that flying small planes long distances can be very tiring as the luxury of an autopilot is not normally fitted, and the Warrior was no exception. However trimming elevator and rudder tabs did help to keep the plane on an even keel for short periods.

The following page shows the crowded Eastern Seaboard from the peace of Northern Virginia, the hustle of the big cities, and forward to Maine, New Brunswick and tranquillity. (Providence airport where I made my landfall is just north of New York).

Q U É B E C
A D A
Notre Dame Mountains
NEW BRUNSWICK
Québec
Laurentian Scarp
MONTREAL
Ottawa
MAINE
VERMONT
NEW HAMPSHIRE
Portland
Portsmouth
Lake Ontario
Rochester
Syracuse
Utica
Albany
NEW YORK
Binghamton
Cape Ann
MASSACHUSETTS
BOSTON
Worcester
Springfield
HARTFORD
PROVIDENCE
CONNECTICUT
RHODE
Cape Cod
Poughkeepsie
New Haven
New London
Martha's Vineyard
Nantucket Island
Block Island
Montauk Point
Scranton
Long Island
Newark
NEW YORK
Allentown
Reading
Harrisburg
NEW
PHILADELPHIA
JERSEY
York
Atlantic City
MARYLAND
BALTIMORE
ATLANTIC
OCEAN
DELAWARE
Cape May
WASHINGTON
Assateague I.
Richmond
Cape Charles

Ahead was the vast metropolis of New York City, the busy sector of airways over the `Big Apple` with the roar of jet engines from the multitude of airliners all around the sky. I quickly concentrated on flying; especially as the weather was a little `iffy`. I started to listen for them to call out my registration and integration into the system and fought to understand the constant gabble on the radio. Fortunately the American Air Traffic Controllers are extremely helpful and will warn you of dodgy weather ahead, especially if the plane in which you are flying does not have weather radar installed. Cruising in cloud and unable to see something unpleasant lurking in the gloom can be quite disconcerting.

At the time there was good visibility, but there were some towering turbulent cumulus clouds around. This meant I had to take a meandering course, along with many airliners whose pilots were sensibly thinking of their passengers and not wanting to give them a rough ride. I take my hat off to the Air Traffic staff *(if I had one on)*, as it could not have been easy with three large International Airports beneath us -JFK, Newark and LaGuardia. They had to look after both the incoming and departing planes, along with nuisances such as myself routing overhead the airports. The east side of the States can get pretty crowded, and I could not wait for the open skies of the northern latitudes. Weather watching can make the difference from an extremely unpleasant and possibly dangerous flight to one of mild discomfort. I was getting a little concerned with regard to the increase in turbulence and strong wind forecast, so I decided to give the rest of New York a wide berth and go direct to Boston. Though judging by the bad weather ahead, I was not sure whether even that was advisable: the eastern Atlantic seaboard is notorious for its extremes of weather. Anyone who has been there can testify to the incredible temperature variations of intense heat and cold, of deep snow and torrential flooding: caused by massive weather systems meeting the might of the Atlantic.

Boston International – Closed

On the radio there was an announcement that due to a super severe thunderstorm Boston-Logan Airport was closed, so I had to decide quickly where I would land. Apparently, this was due to lightning strikes, hail, heavy rain showers and severe wind shear all in the same storm. Whilst it is not common to close a major airport, it does seem to be happening more often. In the distance we saw a huge cumulous nimbus thundercloud, which was so large that the Boeing 747 ahead looked like a miniature aircraft. If you put your thumb on the windscreen, the 747 would disappear but the solitary cloud would still fill the horizon. The thunderstorm is bad enough but compound that with severe wind shear, airframe icing (*which reduces the lift and aerodynamic stability especially when coming into land*), plus torrential rain, and you have a big problem. Sometimes when planes skid off the runway the weather is blamed as the `baddy`, but often the pilots should not have attempted a landing in the first place.

Clouds that are perhaps eight to ten miles high can have freezing rain/hail pouring out of the bottom near ground level. Dragging downwards an ice-cold wind from the stratosphere at minus 50 centigrade and travelling very fast, you can begin to understand the frightening reality of a loaded thunderstorm. The battle of the giants begins and Mother Nature is at war!

With all the schedule airliners jockeying in line for onward clearances to their alternate airport this puts an enormous pressure on the Traffic Controllers. They have to re-direct many aircraft in a matter of minutes – so I opted out of the Airways system. Pushing the Warrior's control yoke forward and turning it to the right in a gentle bank, I descended low level heading towards the impressive Statue of Liberty before going eastward over Long Island and away from the crowded skies.

The 10,000 Ton Cloud

Someone once said to me – why fly? Flying big planes is bad enough, but flying small fragile planes a long way is dangerous. In reply, I spoke of a certain conversation that was held some 2,000 years ago, between a person named Taikung Jen, and the truly original philosopher Confucius.

"I'll teach you how to escape death", Confucius said. "There is a raven in the eastern Sea which is called Yitai (dullhead). This dull-head cannot fly very high and seems very stupid. It hops only a short distance and nestles close with the others of its kind. In going forward, it dare not lead, and in going back, it dare not lag behind. At the time of feeding, it takes what is left over by the other birds. Therefore, the ranks of this bird are never depleted and nobody can do them any harm. A tree with a straight trunk is the first to be chopped down, a well with sweet water is the first to be drawn dry."

Maybe the Yitai will lead a long life, but it does make you think. Preferring the pioneering spirit of adventure, if death comes along I would merely punch it on the nose and carry on.

Pretty but dangerous – thank goodness for weather radar (photo by Thor, God of Thunder!).

Clouds are heavier than you think! The average large cumulus cloud can weigh several hundred tons and collectively many thousands! All that water vapour contains something like 10,000,000,000 drops of water per cubic metre. A very large group of thunderstorms can let loose an incredible 125 million gallons of water, so you can begin to understand the power of nature. Imagine you are driving through an intense storm with the rain falling in bucket loads, the road is say 4 inches *(100mm)* deep in water. If you include the area to the side, behind, and in front, each of the countless buckets of water would weigh around 8.5 lbs *(3.8 kilos)* which works out at several hundred thousand tons - providing my maths are correct. Someone very brainy once calculated that at any one time there is in excess of several hundred million tons of water vapour in the atmosphere at any one time! You can appreciate why Pilots will do anything to keep out of these truly water locked clouds, to avoid the turbulence and potential severe damage.

A positive attribute of rain is that it cleanses the atmosphere of impurities whilst the down side is drowning people and flooding their houses. Once it has washed out those pollutants, rain is very good for washing your hair and makes it all shiny and silky! Though I have yet to see hoards of people running around, jumping with glee and foaming at the head. Depending on where you are in the world, you could have a really hot shower or turn slowly into a block of ice.

Skies would be boring without the fluffy clumps of clouds whose shapes equally match those of a kaleidoscope – forever changing – inside out and outside in - never the same. Folklore tells us that at the end of a rainbow there is a pot of gold for that lucky person who finds the multi-coloured finish, but I have yet to meet anyone who has! A marvellously written book by Gavin Pretor-Pinney called, appropriately enough, The Cloudspotter's Guide, is an excellent foray into the world of clouds and rainbows.

So, with Mother Nature in her element giving us lightning flashes and deafening thunderclaps, and with Boston being closed, an immediate landing in a small airport was the best option. Besides, with a long flight, tiredness was coming on and a good rest for the night was definitely needed. Providence, Rhode Island Airport was my alternative. It was pretty much the size of Gatwick Airport but with fewer passenger terminal buildings. I still had not got used to just how big the USA is, and how large are their `provincial` airports. I used less than 20% of the runway to land the little Piper Warrior!

 Invariably there is an abundance of hotels vying for business and Providence was no exception. A limo collected us from the airport terminal; the cost being included in the inexpensive rate for the room. The Boston lobster meal we enjoyed cost more than the accommodation! The area was not particularly exciting, but adequate, and it was only a few hours flight from Moncton, which was to be our next stop for Customs clearance, and for that all important equipment and licence check. Because the east coast of America faces Europe it is from here on the

134

eastern Seaboard that there have been so many attempts at reaching the other side of the `pond`.

Denis as I will always remember him, enjoying Lobster and getting into a deep conversation about flying. (Photo taken by David Robinson and reproduced with his permission).

It was north of here, in Nova Scotia, that a less well-known intrepid aviator landed. Beryl Markham who had flown in 1936 from Abingdon *(Oxford)* Airport to mainland USA wrote the book `West with the Night.` As Ernest Hemingway said, `*A bloody wonderful book!*` I thought that it was very well written and an extremely interesting and marvellous story, with her descriptions of flying Tiger Moths around Kenya, to flying all the way to England, and then back down again through Africa. She was deeply involved with the social elite of Kenya, England and finally America where she was to live for some years. Her romantic involvements caused many scandals and included some famous film stars, as well as British Royalty.

Beryl Markham started flying in the late 1920's around the mines of Kenya, the Sudan, Tanganyika and Rhodesia taking mail and supplies to the men, and even flying the sick to hospital one at a time in the small bi-plane. She was exceptionally brave and had no hesitation in going forth into the unknown. In 1936 she made world headlines by becoming the first person to fly solo against the prevailing winds across the Atlantic Ocean from east to west. She made the journey in 21 hours 25 minutes in a British Percival Vega Gull with a De Havilland Gipsy engine constructed and modified for the flight. As with many other pioneers her name has disappeared into the dust of history, and to read her autobiography opens a world that has gone forever. In those days the privileged were few and they travelled the same circles together, from famous European ski slopes to the shores of the Caribbean. Their world encompassed London, Paris, the Cote d`Azur, Monte Carlo, Rome, New York, Los Angeles, and last but certainly not least, Hollywood. It was truly a playground of the richest few, many of whom had a life style which was one of continuous debauchery – that word in the dictionary covers just about everything you could possibly think of plus some more!

Flying against the prevailing winds can be quite *"dodgy"*, an increase in head wind can mean running out of fuel. Something I had to be very aware of when crossing large expanses of water. In the pioneering days rescues seldom happened, in part due to the time between the incident and the few days later when someone realised that a person was missing. Also in part due to lack of communication, as it was not unknown for a pilot to land on a mere whim of choice somewhere totally different to that planned. Beryl did not quite make New York as unfortunately she had some problems with the plane, luckily over land, and had to make an emergency landing in smelly swampy fields only a few miles from the safety of Sydney Airport, Nova Scotia. Once again the word ice comes up; the engine had picked up some icing in the fuel vent pipe and just quit running. If she had to ditch an hour or so earlier in the cold Atlantic, no one would have known the cause – perhaps blaming the innocent reliable engine for her demise? Apparently, she was quite angry at landing in a bog, but was more annoyed at the state of her clothes, rather than realising she had just made history! Beryl got to New York eventually, and was hailed as a heroine for her remarkable achievement.

There were many very courageous and adventurous people in the early days of flying. It was a very dubious time for those brave enough to leave Mother Earth; unreliable parachutes and no proper seat belts - come to that, some planes did not even have seats! Tied up with cloth, wire and string, with flimsy wooden spars, in the beginning flying machines were a disaster waiting to happen. Despite this there were more pioneering heroic flying attempts and adventures, especially long distance trans-ocean and trans-continental journeys, in the 20`s and 30`s than in any other age even to the present day. The progress made during that turbulent time paved the way ahead.

The Highest Tide In The World Hop

Departing from Providence in the little Warrior the following morning, and with more bad weather in front of us, I headed northeast towards our destination of Moncton, New Brunswick. Flying up the Bay of Fundy the waters of which have the greatest tide range in the world, my descending turn towards the airport took us low level over these potentially extremely dangerous waters. There are great variations of tides in the world, some benign and just a couple of feet as in the Caribbean, with others in less hospitable locations at 20 or 30 feet. Nevertheless, none so extreme as The Bay of Fundy

Hopewell Rocks, towards the top of the Bay – the lower level will be under 50 foot of water in a few hours – hence the raised platform where at high tide people can stand without getting their feet wet. The rocks look like ancient trees where the rushing tide has eroded the bases. (photo courtesy of New Brunswick Tourism).

The Bay is 290 kilometres long, *(approx 180 miles)* and the mouth of the Bay 100 kilometres wide *(approx 62 miles)* and around 200 metres *(600 feet)* deep. Basically a funnel shaped area which narrows towards the end of the inlet to 2.5 kilometres *(1.5 miles)* with a depth of 14 metres *(45 feet)*. Thereon splitting to form Chignecto Bay and the Minas Basin. Becoming increasingly shallower, the water divides into Shepody Bay. Unusual names, but then the whole area is littered with ancient and once upon a time meaningful names. The highest tides of the Bay are due to a unique local factor. The gradual tapering and reduction of depth constricts the tidal flow. This causes the waters to rise from an average of 1 metre *(3 feet)* throughout the world to the 16 metre *(52 feet)* tidal range found at the end of the Bay. This meshing of the two systems means that the tidal range is amplified. I always wondered why there were so many tourists in such a small town as Moncton and now I know the reason: a set of rocks and a Bay called Fundy. To see the sea roaring past like an express train is something not to be missed.

Try sitting in your bath without getting my book wet, start sloshing the water against the side, keep up the same pressure/movement and you will notice that apart from the floor getting wet the height of your `wave` becomes slightly larger with every movement – this is called the *`Seiche Effect`*. Various unusual or impressive happenings including bore waves, tsunami, freak waves and extreme tides can all in part be attributed to this effect, so bring your swimming costume along and prepare to get very wet.

With a last glimpse at the Bay, I landed the Piper Warrior at Moncton. Meeting up with Customs and the safety check team, we went through the documents and equipment process. Moncton Airport being close to mainland USA and on the east coast was a perfect location for this clearance. It has been known for the odd inexperienced private pilot, with a mind to cross to Greenland, to get all the way to Goose Bay in Labrador, and then the Canadian Authorities would impound the plane because of the lack of the correct type of survival gear or licence. The pilot would then be sent scurrying back to the warm south. After several fatal accidents, the Authorities were not taking any more chances.

The following map shows the area flown from Providence airport south of Boston, Maine, passing Novia Scotia, the Bay of Fundy and to Moncton Airport, New Brunswick. Onward it was a detour to Quebec, Sept Isles and to Goose Bay, Labrador. From there the flight would leave mainland North America heading to Greenland.

NEWFOUNDLAND
LABRADOR
QUÉBEC
Plateau Laurentien
Churchill Falls
Tunungayualok I.
C. Makkovik
C. Harrison
Belle Isle
Old Post Pt.
Jacques Cartier Passage
Anticosti I.
East Pt.
Honguedo Passage
Gaspé
Notre Dame Mts.
Pen.
C. Gaspé
GULF OF
ST. LAWRENCE
St. Lawrence
Shippigan I.
C. St. George
C. Ray
Cabot Strait
C. North
Long Range Mts.
Newfoundland
Grande Miquelon
(France)
Petite Miquelon
(France)
St. Pierre
(France)
St. Pierre
Bank
Québec
NEW
BRUNSWICK
PRINCE EDWARD
ISLAND
East Pt.
Cape Breton I.
Glace Bay
C. Breton
MONTRÉAL
MAINE
NOVA SCOTIA
Halifax
Grand
Manan I.
Mt. Desert I.
VT.
N.H.

I tracked down an engineer who would be responsible for putting in the HF radio aerial. He laughingly suggested in a friendly sort of way that if he put a couple of hooks on the bottom of the 40-foot long cable that was to be trailed out of the bottom of the plane, I could fly low over the sea and catch a few fish! Mind you, that idea was fraught with problems, for instance, how could we cook them? In addition, the fish would be temptingly bobbing around a couple of feet under the plane with no way of retrieval! Safety wise I would need to remember to wind in the steel wire prior to landing, and perhaps there would be a chance that a fish might still be hanging there.

There was also the regulation about having two ADF *(automatic direction finders)* fitted. This was 1988 just before every man and his dog went mad on GPS *(global positioning system)*. The portable ADF used in earlier trips was a back up as it is really easy to get lost further north. Incidentally, the ADF was in operation some 60 years prior to our flight – so it was not exactly `rocket science`! At the end of the day navigation with a chart, slide rule *(the aviation ones are round for some reason),* a stopwatch and pencil will get you to your destination. My routine check included testing the various navigational instruments and radios, as well as my newly installed portable HF transmitter which was crackling and hissing in the background.

With all the checks completed we were cleared for takeoff, up and away from Moncton direct to Quebec the French speaking capital of the French province. A few months previously in my Company twin-engine plane, I had popped into Quebec as it is a delightful place to stop, so I was looking forward being there again. The first impression one gets when flying into that part of Canada is that everyone is speaking French! It seemed very strange to be in the midst of the great North American Continent and hear a foreign language being spoken between the pilots and Air Traffic Control. It was as if a Tardis time machine had deposited us into the middle of Europe.

The City has around five hundred thousand inhabitants, though surprisingly enough, if you include the whole region there are some seven and a half million; the majority living to the west of Quebec. Still not enough to have someone hiding behind every bush out in the wilderness! It is, after all, a big country, and certainly a wonderful area to live for those who still have a pioneering spirit and enjoy camping in its true basic form. As we flew I noticed the land was starting to become more sparsely populated. Quebec City is the last densely inhabited area we would encounter until we reached Iceland.

The (French) Canadian Hop

Coming towards Quebec airport the weather turned quite sour and we landed to squally rain showers. Fortunately, the airport is well equipped with full bad weather instrument landing systems. I put my faith in a pair of 15-year-old instruments, which indicated the way to go, left or right, and up or down. The crosshairs ever converging into a point indicating the runway was still in front of the nose. I had to fly blind down the glide path until breaking out of the cloud where happily the runway appeared in front of us. After landing I turned onto the taxiway where there appeared a little van which had yellow lights flashing with a `follow me` sign, guiding us to the aircraft park in front of the tower. This seemed a trifle excessive as Quebec has only one runway and could hardly be classed as big. However it kept people employed and that is a good omen. My cousin Jason was there to meet us wrapped up as if it were a cold December day; ok it had been raining pretty hard, but it was summer!

We drove downtown through the usual hubbub of city traffic. Our hotel was as boring as most lodge type places are these days but what a transformation when going out into the metropolis. A lot of loving care and thought has gone into the restoration of the old city, packed with lots of super restaurants set in a Parisian ambiance, and very friendly natives or should I say local inhabitants? It is odd that one minute everyone is speaking French and then they suddenly burst into strongly accented English. The difference between European French and Canadian French is that one is fairly easy to understand, whilst the other almost impossible until one gets used to the accent. On the north side of the City there is a very large underground shopping mall, so in winter with lots of snow on the ground, one is able to window shop in the warm. There is also an imposing university standing impressively in its own grounds, with students from lots of cultural backgrounds and nationalities.

The following day sitting in a café overlooking the mighty St Lawrence river was something quite special, and you could go back in time with the ramparts of Quebec City still surrounding the castle. This is what the British General Wolfe would have seen when he sailed up the river. James Wolfe was one of the leaders of the expedition sent to seize French Canada, and he played a vital role in the capture of Louisbourg on Cape Breton Island in 1758. The following year he commanded the attack on the French capital, the city of Quebec. Unfortunately, fatally wounded whilst leading his troops to victory on the Plains of Abraham, he never saw the battle that was to lead to British control of Canada. All rather sad really as the British already had a good relationship with the Canadians – but then politicians always seem to screw up something that was working fine before they butted into the scene.

Whilst the City has undoubtedly changed, the view of the river and beyond is today as it was all those years ago. Fortunately, the Quebecians have forgiven the British - or at least they were very friendly to us! As Quebec is still a pioneering City, many people at the weekends pack a bag and tent and just drive off into the interior. There they find spread out before them the wilderness that would have presented itself to the approaching British Forces in the eighteenth century.

Whilst we were spending a couple of days enjoying the culinary delights of French cuisine, the plane was having the main ADF repaired. It had been previously checked ok at Moncton, but for some reason it just stopped working. This somewhat old-fashioned instrument pointed towards a navigational beacon and was used equally by ships and planes. As a sideline, the ADF working on the mw/lw frequencies was capable of picking up general radio programmes. As such, it was quite possible to listen to some music whilst navigating, though attempting to listen through the buzzes, hisses, and bleeps that the navigation beacon was giving out made it barely worth the effort. An added problem was that it would not take into consideration direction or wind, so a certain amount of scribbling on the chart was required to fly the correct heading. Unfortunately, the avionics company in Quebec did not repair the unit correctly, as it transpired later that somehow they had managed to get the needle pointing 180 degrees out of line. Fortunately the portable receiver, much to our amazement, actually worked.

Goose Bay, Labrador, Canada with Denis in his bright orange survival suit. You can see the 45 gallon red fuel drum just behind the front seat. Behind the Warrior you can see Brian, another ferry pilot. He is flying back a Piper Arrow. Faster with its bigger turbo engine and retractable undercarriage he beat us to Greenland by a couple of hours. It was he who would eventually fly Denis's Cessna 336 back to the UK. (photo by author).

There were also two VHF direction units fitted in the plane which were much easier to use, and pointed the precise heading to the beacon. Slight problem here was there were very few beacons that worked on the VOR/VHF frequency - in part due to the limited range, and the cost of maintenance of this sensitive equipment in such a harsh environment. The ADF had a range of several hundred miles or more *(with limitations),* and was cheaper to maintain, whereas the VOR/VHF unit realistically had a range of up to 120 miles depending on altitude. The last piece of navigational help was the Loran. Comparable to an early form of a GPS it was unfortunately quite unreliable in certain geographic locations. For instance it would be useless crossing the most awkward parts of our northern journey i.e. the Arctic Ocean. At one point on the journey, to save on weight I thought of throwing it out of the plane, but as we did not have any large opening windows that idea was soon shelved.

A Further North Hop

Talking of equipment I must mention the 1940 ARCTIC SURVIVAL BOOK, which was issued to the wartime Canadian and American aircrews flying into the northern latitudes and across the Atlantic Ocean. This booklet was sent to me only a few years ago by the Canadian Government *(nice to know that they are keeping up with the times!).* It is incredibly boring in some parts, so blatantly obvious in others, and such a mind boggling confusion of words in other sections that it defies belief. Read the extracts on the following pages and you will see what I mean. We were amazed that anyone managed to get across to Great Britain without losing hope *(or their mind)* after reading the so-called survival information. Indeed, one would have had to take a large suitcase to put in all the equipment the booklet suggested; plus a translator to unravel the words. I wouldn`t want to belittle any form of survival information, but I would love to have met the person who wrote the Articles. I cherish the bit in the manual about finding the Southern Cross; which would have been a might difficult bearing in mind that particular constellation is in the Southern Hemisphere! Hopefully whoever did the editing would have brought the book up to date, but that seemed not to have happened.

The following *(amusing)* extracts are taken from the 1940 Arctic Survival Booklet *(as originally printed)*.

Footwear
(a) The Mukluk Assembly is worn instead of flying boots by aircrew operating in dry cold conditions (that is unless you have to ditch in the sea). It consists of:
(i) Three pairs of woollen socks sized to fit over one another without creasing.
(ii) A duffle sock made of blanketing and sized to fit effectively over the woollen socks.
(iii) A thick felt insole with a ventilating mesh sole, worn downwards, to provide effective insulation beneath the foot.

(iv) A Mukluk, which has a waterproof canvas upper extending over the calf and a rubber sole and galosh. The sole is ribbed for good traction on snow. The top of the boot can be closed by a draw cord.

(b) The Boucheron is worn by personnel operating in wet cold conditions. This boot has a leather waterproof upper extending to just below the knee and a rubber sole and galosh. It is unlined but has a removable felt insole. It may be worn over the woollen socks and duffle sock as required.

What I cannot understand is, what happens if you are going to ditch? Do you change your boots? If so, to what? As there is no mention of any other type of footwear. Lastly the following:

In order to prevent frostbite on the face, the `downed aircrew` will need to continuously make faces by moving the mouth from side to side.

At least it might have amused the Polar bear whilst deciding which part of you to eat first.

The brain fairly boggles at the thought, but goodness knows what I would have done if I had to use the book for real! However, armed with the `essential` survival manuscript, we set off into the unknown. Well that's what they say in books........

Departing Quebec City we needed to fly up the River Lawrence to Sept Isles Airport for a last refuel before Goose Bay on the northeast tip of Labrador, and the Arctic Ocean. Coincidently it was lunchtime, and as we were getting a little fed up with in flight sandwiches, the decision was made to have a proper meal when we arrived before heading further north.

Several hours later I received clearance to land at Sept Isles Airport, harmoniously squashed between the settlement on the banks of the River Lawrence, and a large forest on the landside of the runway. Parking the plane on the apron and closing down the engine the peace was so noticeable that we did not want to speak. The abundance of trees dotted around the lakes was an amazing sight. Beauty is all around - and remote areas seem to supply spectacular scenery. In autumn there is a magnificent spread of colours due to the variety of trees. Hues of greens, browns and golden orange abound, with all the blends in between, like an ever changing kaleidoscope.

Across the water was the Gaspè Peninsula with Anticosti Island pointing towards Newfoundland and ultimately Ireland and the UK. The famous Gaspè Peninsula was named after the son of a distinguished Quebec family. Philippe Aubert de Gaspè *(1786-1871)* inherited the family estate (*some estate*) on the St. Lawrence River. He received a classic education in Quebec, studied law there, and later became sheriff. Bankruptcy, due to overspending and poor

152

management, for which he spent over three years in debtors prison, forced him, in his 40's, to withdraw from the public scene, and lead a quiet life of reading and meditation. In 1863 when he was the ripe old age of 76 and inspired by a rebirth of Canadian Nationalism, he wrote `Les Anciens Canadiens`, which became a French-Canadian classic. It is a romantic historical novel set in Canada at the time of the British Conquest of 1760. The Gaspè Peninsula is now a huge and happy conservation area, so that today everyone can enjoy this wonderful place.

Whilst looking eastwards towards home, I wistfully thought of the straight-easterly route from Gander on the island of Newfoundland to Shannon in Ireland. It is a popular route for larger aircraft, and the odd small plane specially fitted with a very large extra fuel tank; but was not possible in our case. Besides which, I wanted to go further north and re-visit Greenland. Gander Airport is one of the most famous airports on the eastern side of the United States & Canada. Numerous passenger planes in earlier times used both Gander and Shannon as stop off and refuel bases for the limited endurance of the older airliners.

Shannon airport had the reputation of having one of the largest and best-stocked Duty Free shops in the world. Regulations stipulated that all passengers must disembark whilst refuelling. Therefore, they had captive passengers running round the enormous Duty Free buying up their bargains before carrying on to sunny Florida and other destinations. Quite often they had to land there again on the way back, depending on the strength of the jet stream. Needless to say, when the airliners became more fuel efficient Shannon lost its customers and never recovered.

Apart from a refuelling stop, Gander is also a very important rescue centre owing to its prominent position jutting out into the Atlantic Ocean. Many famous films were made in this part of the world including *The Shipping News* and *The Perfect Storm*, both superb in their own way. Though after seeing *The Perfect Storm* I'm sure that it would put off anyone sailing a long way in a small boat. It would certainly not be the ideal choice for an Ocean liner to put on as the Saturday night special feature film! I guess similar to flying – a happy movie has to be better than one that makes for nervous passengers. Both films show how brave were the fishermen in bygone times - and indeed still are - working their vessels in the notorious *Newfoundland Banks*. In the whaling times there were scores of whalers that set sail from those shores, many never to see their homes again. Not too far away the Titanic came to her tragic and premature end on her first voyage. It was 400 miles south of Newfoundland in 1912, that the luxury liner collided with an iceberg with the loss of some 1500 souls.

Fishing is part of the way of life in these remote areas; having little industry, the inhabitants have scant choice. If you asked the fishermen if they would prefer a different occupation, I am sure that many would prefer a safer job working on land, and getting back to their families each evening. It makes you wonder sometimes how people living in these isolated and desolate places can make a livelihood. Just by flying around in a little plane in the more inaccessible areas you were, for a while, part of their existence. You have a fleeting glimpse of how tough and different their world is from the modern hustle and bustle of our cities and towns.

I was on an aborted ferry trip to collect a Cessna 206 when I took this photo in Anchorage, Alaska, north west USA of the wonderful everlasting, ever ready, and as you can see, ever so cold, De Havilland Beaver.

The airliners travelling inter-city may share the same skies as little planes, but they cannot make the same short hops from their height and they do not have the same visual connection with the ground; which often is breathtakingly beautiful. They therefore miss all that is revealed to people in small planes. Mind you, in many instances when the weather is really bad low down, there are times when I have wished to be able to go to a higher altitude!

Flying a light aircraft is the best way to see the world. On occasions you need a strong stomach when trying local culinary dishes, but believe me it is really worth the effort. Over the 3 weeks taken on this trip, Denis and I munched and drank our way through some unusual and tasty dishes, as well encountering some interesting people. A friendly greeting was commonplace wherever we went and quite a few commented on why we were making a long and hazardous trip in such a little plane. I just smiled and said. *"The pioneering era isn't over, and it sure beats the hell out of sitting in the back of a Jumbo jet"*.

Onward North Hop Through Newfoundland/Labrador

After refuelling the Warrior and enjoying a meal of fresh fish from the Lawrence river, we departed yet another historical area. We said goodbye to the friendly Sept Isles Air Traffic Control, and flew a low graceful arc over Anticosti Island in a sweeping turn pointing north-by-north east towards Goose Bay. The port wing skimmed the trees, like a scythe that could not quite reach. After Sept Isles, the land becomes really barren, with lots of small lakes in a series of hillocks, some green, some brown and most covered in lichen; with water and ice lying in the dips. There were few places to land except on the more open tundra which would have taken out the undercarriage had the need arose to curtail the flight. Indeed the best plane to operate in this area is the ubiquitous amphibious seaplane. Though in this part of Labrador most of the *"lakes"* were too small for landing anything but a micro-light. When I had been in Alaska checking out a Cessna 206, I noted that there were more floatplanes than any other type.

Labrador may seem a part of east Canada but it is in a league of its own. It is a vast predominately uninhabited area larger than England and Wales, with only a few brave people living there. It had hardly been explored before the 19th century and even then only in very small regions. The summer season is very brief and in the far north only lasting 3 months or so. But do not think about going then, winter - as cold as it is with icy gales screaming down from the north - is a better time.

In the clammy summer, there is an invasion of the most voracious flying insects known to man; from the humble midge *(no se ums)* which bite like fury, to the unbearable swarms of mosquito. Then Black Fly that actually bite chunks of flesh from your body. They are the scourge of livestock, causing weight loss in cattle and in some cases, death. Further west, add on the warble fly and the nose bot fly, which seem to attack the migrating Caribou more than other creatures. Last but not least is the horse fly *(strange name as there are few horses to be found)* commonly known as the `Bull Dog`. This creature from hell is possessed by a blood thirst that can only be discouraged by sudden death! All these insects cause untold misery to anyone and anything in that inhospitable land – people, bears, wolves, birds, moose, caribou, the list goes on – there are no exceptions. Though most of the Canadian northern territories suffer from this onslaught of insects, it seems than Labrador gets more than its share of these pests. Stories have been told of some animals which will run off the edge of a cliff in blind panic to rid themselves of these evil bugs. The swarms get so large that they can literally drive you insane. There is an old wives tale that implies an extremely cold winter is good to kill off the bugs. Do not believe it! The winter may kill you off but these little devils seem to survive in any extreme of temperature.

Goose Bay, Labrador Canada, my camouflaged survival suit which would blend into the Atlantic Ocean and therefore guarantee my slim chance of survival being even slimmer! Note the dark hair which rapidly turned a shade of grey during the flight! (Photo by Denis).

When we were just past the point of no return with no radio contact to the outside world, Goose Bay seemed an awful long way to go, but I pondered on the weird and wonderful names we were encountering. I wonder who ever thought of calling an airport in a wild and remote part of the Newfoundland coast line `Goose Bay` and indeed was he or she related to the person naming the other airport further south `Gander`? Mind you, when we eventually got to Goose we were booked into a lodge in the `Happy Valley` community. I have to say that the mind fairly boggled as to what we would find when we arrived. As the airport was military, we had to go into the full approach to land procedure by radar vectors, which was probably just as well with poor visibility and a few military jets buzzing around.

The airport terminal was quite small but had a very long runway to accommodate the larger military aircraft and was covered in skid marks from the landing fighters. The larger Armed Forces section was out of bounds for civilian use. The Forward Defence Command at Goose Bay was very noticeable. Now and then some very loud combatant plane would fly low on manoeuvres and destroy the beautiful peace and tranquillity. I find it rather sad that the military have to disturb the serenity with their incredibly loud machines. At least our little plane was hardly noticeable, with the sound equating more to a lawnmower when compared to the loud roar of a jet.

It was interesting to see that at the entrance to the military camp there was standing as a `gate guardian`, an old Gloster Javelin, one of the very early post war British fighter jets. Evidently there is quite a large Royal Air Force presence in this isolated spot. In the terminal building there were numerous civilians, mainly trappers and seriously minded explorers. Beards were the `in thing` so I was pleased that I had not shaved mine off when we were in sunnier climes. Certainly, some of the clothing people were wearing seemed to indicate that they were expecting a serious drop in temperature, whilst others were dressed for a beach stroll. I guess at the end of the day some were bound for Happy Valley whilst others were heading for the outback. The Goose Bay community or perhaps I should say `Happy Valley,` is a very close-knit fishing settlement and they are cautiously friendly. As long as you are there to eat their fish from the few little eating places, and not there to compete with their meagre existence, then all is well. Not the place to get out a fishing rod and sit on the end of the rickety old pier, as there was every chance you would end up under it!

Our sleeping lodge was down a rough rutted track with the odd snow bike rusting on the side of the verge. It appears that even here when something breaks downs it becomes dumped garbage: sadly modern debris is everywhere. The lodge had triple glazed windows in view of the cold winters experienced in those northern latitudes. That was fine last time when I was there in the cool autumn, but quite unbearable in the summer, as it was so hot inside, and there was no way of opening a window.

Spending a while at the bar, we got talking to the locals and a mix of tourists, some of whom were visiting their friends and family. There were also the dedicated bird watching groups who seem to manifest themselves everywhere, along with a few prospectors - some of whom seemed to think that the bar was prospect enough! A few explorers and a couple of soldiers from the military camp made up the rest. We got onto the touchy subject of seal slaughtering – something we should have avoided, especially as we support the poor seal cubs. Do not mention the word `seals` if you want to get out of a bar in one piece, especially when there are several burly fishermen in attendance. Denis managed to divert the subject by a couple of well-timed jokes – along with buying a round of drinks - and all was back to normal.

After a very large reindeer steak and chips in the lodge's restaurant, I hid in a corner of the room for some peace, and considered the route planning of the journey. This ongoing task requires very careful deliberation due to the vagaries of weather and destination facilities. We studied the latest weather synopsis chart to see what nature had in store for us.

The flying part in some ways is the least of the problems; with a well-prepared machine in good mechanical order the pilot has time to consider the outside influences with a more relaxed mind. Magnetic variation throughout the world affects the compass and in the UK and surrounding Europe, it is only 4 or 5 degrees. By way of a comparison, the magnetic variation between Canada and southern

Greenland varies as much as 45 degrees depending on the Latitude *(even more further north)*. This is a serious amount of error; plotting a course and entering variation correctly into the equation is paramount to survival *(and that is no joke)*.

The Earth's north magnetic pole at the moment is located in northeast Canada, about 600 km from the nearest town Resolute Bay, around 1,500 kilometres northwest of southern Greenland. The population of around 300 souls apparently wear a popular T-shirt which reads, `*Resolute Bay isn't the end of the world, but you can see it from here*`. Bleak, boring and b***** cold is the term I have heard used about Resolute Bay! I doubt if the T-shirt Company makes very much profit on the sales. It is normally so cold in this part of the globe I wonder who actually sees the T-shirts - which are probably buried under half a dozen thick woolly sweaters.

Quite a distance from the real North Pole the magnetic north does not stay in one place; following the magna core deep inside our planet, the compass merely indicates its approximate position. Prior to the GPS navigators used a special form of navigation called sensibly enough Grid Navigation, breaking big areas into useable squares.

Another observation worthy of noting is the dip in the compass. The nearer one gets to magnetic north the more the compass wants to point into the earth. Something to watch out for as it can render useless such an important item. You can imagine – every time you want to check the compass you would have to put the plane into a nosedive – read the heading and then quickly pull up the control column. Normally compasses need special adjustment for this part of the world but as we were only passing through, careful monitoring was all that was required.

As with other navigators, I had to take into account the deviation of the plane. Any ferrous metal within the cockpit affects the compass. However some clever engineer has worked out a set of deviation tables. A small printed card showing the changes in the heading is placed by the compass. Depending on the heading there will be a plus or minus of several degrees which needs to be included in the overall calculation.

It really all goes for `a ball of chalk` when you realise that upon heading for true north from southern Greenland, when passing magnetic north, the compass will actually point towards south *(i.e. behind you)* depending on your route to the pole. Coming from the other side of the world you can actually fly over the North Pole with the compass still pointing straight ahead.

The compass only indicates magnetic north so you need to plot a course depending on your heading from magnetic north to get to true north. Add the fact that the north pole does not stay still (*unlike the Antarctic where the pole is firmly fixed*) but meanders at the whim of the currents in the Arctic Ocean, it is a wonder that anyone can find the place! We all know that the Arctic is a great big blob of snow and ice *(effectively frozen water)* surrounded by land. Conversely the Antarctic is land covered in ice and snow and surrounded by water.

Imagine for a moment that an estate agent came along with a view *(pardon the pun)* to a deal, and asked if you would like to buy some unspoilt land on top of the world; with a panoramic view of the sea. Do not say yes to the North Pole; sadly it will one day become all water and your money would have gone down the drain. However say yes to the South Pole, as it will one day be rich in valleys and mountains *(apart from tons of penguin poo!)* when all the snow disappears.

With all our sophisticated wonders of communication, magnetism rules the world. Without it we would not be able to navigate or communicate, and our phones would be rendered useless; along with computers, radio and television. Even the fish and birds would get hopelessly lost, and I guess you can include me in that. Last but not least, the sun's solar flares would destroy the earth's atmosphere. The worst scenario in our case would be that instead of heading toward Greenland, we would be taking a pretty much direct course to Spain, or conversely direct to the real North Pole and Father Christmas! That would be fine but with 2,000 plus miles to cross, and nothing but ice and snow or the Atlantic Ocean in the way, either route would be a disaster. Even with the survival suits that we wore, there was slim chance of surviving in such an inhospitable sea. We would have to get into the liferaft within a few minutes of ditching; otherwise our muscles would have ceased working due to the intense cold and we would be incapable of climbing into it. Rescue was nigh on impossible. The `Jolly Green Giant Helicopters` flown by the American Rescue teams would barely have the range to reach you, let alone hover around trying to find someone in waves 20 foot high or more. The route to the North Pole would have been as bad, just freezing in snow instead of water; or being eaten by a hungry Polar bear.

On a more cheerful note, with the Piper Warrior refuelled and made ready for the Arctic Ocean flight. I sorted out my flight plan, checked the weather and then we did a little sightseeing in Goose Bay. Nearby there is still one of the old Hudson Bay Trading posts. Even now, it is possible to trade in pelts for food and supplies. We let the side down by buying a couple of bars of chocolate; no fur coats or Beaver hats for us.

There were very few vehicles around except for the odd ever-ready taxi car. There was little point in owning a vehicle as there were no real roads, just a few tracks to the occasional outlying settlement. However, since I was previously in Goose Bay progress sadly has found its way there. I understand that at certain times of the year one can drive with a suitable 4x4 vehicle to Quebec City - no doubt a long and extremely arduous journey; and camping en route would be fraught with problems.

According to historians The Hudson's Bay Company started in the 1600`s, initially in Fort York near the Hudson and spreading outwards. It was a French idea, not British as most people assume. The Company was begun by two French Canadians named Radisson and Groseilliers - food for thought - as amusingly enough their names roughly translate as Radish and Gooseberry,!

One of the many furs the Hudson Bay Company traded in was Beaver. King Charles 1st decreed in the 17th Century that all fur hats must be made of Beaver; presumably he had shares or trapping rights to Beavers! Because the fur was expensive, some ingenious person started making them out of Rabbit fur and treated it with a mercury based potion to give that Beaver *"feel"*. Unfortunately, the mercury poisoned the poor workers by being absorbed through the skin. This produced serious brain disorders – hence the well known saying `Mad As a Hatter` – look it up in `*Through The Looking Glass with Alice In Wonderland*`. Needless to say Beavers were driven to the brink of extinction. This in turn created other problems; the loss of their dam making talents. This made some rivers flow too fast, causing riverbank erosion because of the inflow increase of the smaller tributaries and streams.

I believe the Americans and Canadians are sensitive and sentimental people: not only naming some aircraft after Indian tribes but also after the Beaver. The legendary De Havilland DHC-2 Beaver ferries farmers, explorers, engineers, tourists and all their equipment the length and breadth of Alaska and Canada. The Noorduyn Norseman, DHC-3 Otter, Piper Cub, Cessna Skywagon are all readily adaptable from skis to wheels and a combination of both. All these aircraft fly in the environment of a rugged and unforgiving landscape. Along with other light aircraft, all the Piper models were named after American Indian tribes. These were Warrior, Cherokee, Seneca, Saratoga, Pawnee, Apache, Aztec, Seminole, Comanche, Dakota, and with a slight deviation – Arrow, Archer, Lance. This was a meaningful and thoughtful gesture in order that the proud Indian tribes would not be forgotten. There were also the odd models that had no real following – Aerostar, and the Super Cub.

Cessna did things differently and were very boring in their naming of the various models. They started with a number then tacked on a name - usually sky or wagon: Cessna 336 then 337 with Skymaster on the end followed by 172 Skyhawk, Hawk, Cutlass, 177 Cardinal, 180 Skywagon, 182 Skylane, 206 Stationair, and a 210 Centurion. Therefore, as names go, Piper wins by a large margin. Even the great giant Boeing are as boring as can be with 707,737,727,747,757,777 plus a good few more. The Airbus is the same as Boeing with all its numbers.

Not very exciting is it? Go back a few years and yes you've got it – good old Britain had the following: the De Havilland Venom and Vampire, Hawker Hunter, Avro Lancaster, Spitfire, Hurricane, Bristol Beau fighter, Percival Provost, Handley Page Victor, and the Vulcan. Also the Saunders Roe flying boats and the ultimate flying machine the Concorde. McDonnell Douglas made his contribution with the DC3 (*also called the Dakota*) DC4, DC6, the ill-fated DC10, and the early De Havilland Comet. There are so many more great names but they are too numerous to mention here. Great Britain produced an enormous amount of aircraft – something of which to be proud. Germany's brilliant engineering also produced some excellent planes, including the Dornier, Messerschmitt, Heinkel, Focke-Wulf. There is still the rest of the world – sorry but no more room!

Goose Bay Airport (*our final departure point from mainland North America*) was opened around 1940/41, in order that Canadian and American military & commercial planes could use the base as a transatlantic refuelling stop en route to Europe. By hopping across to Greenland and Iceland it was possible to get to Great Britain and beyond without getting wet feet - unless the aircrew were particularly unlucky with the plane breaking down.

Slightly misleading on the following page, the white area merely shows all the ice and snow that lies within the Arctic Circle. Southern Greenland is also covered in ice and snow.

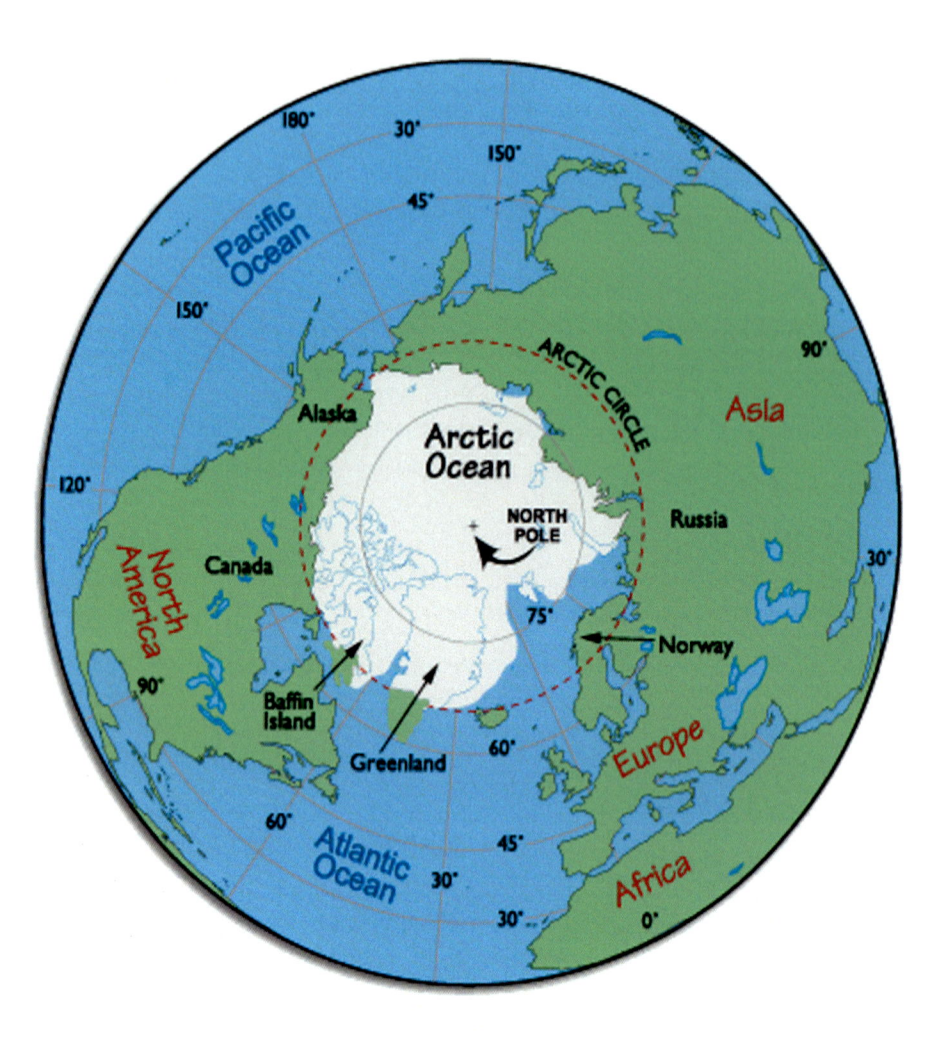

Map courtesy of worldatlas.com.

The name of *Narssarssuaq (or Narsarsuaq depending where you see the spelling)* is the correct title of Greenland's southernmost airport. However for a good many years it was known by the weird and wonderful name of Bluie-West-One. There must be a comedian out there somewhere who thinks up these names because we were preparing for a flight departing Goose Bay and heading to Bluie-West-One, and our back-up contact on the radio was called Sob Story; the mind really boggles! These old names are still used today.

The very fact someone is paid for inventing such bizarre names makes it all the more unbelievable. I would love a job like that. The whole world is full of strange names and maybe one day there will be a book written all about them and their meanings. Canada is criss-crossed with unusual names going back to the various Indian tribes, explorers and settlers.

Where the indigenous Eskimo people are concerned, they are basically divided into two groups with the Inuit in Canada and Greenland, and the Yupik on the American western side of Alaska. It is good that these names remain, thus ensuring the history of the Eskimos will not be forgotten.

Getting ready for departure from Goose Bay, we climbed into our survival/ immersion/dry suits. This is was not some fancy dress outfit to amuse our Eskimo friends, but a submersible costume or perhaps better described as a floatation suit. The idea is to keep you above the waves (*similar to a lifejacket*) and a little bit warmer than the surrounding water, which in our case would be exceedingly cold. In order to continue to exist if we had to `ditch` albeit for a few hours, we needed this costume. Difficult to put on but it keeps you dry inside. The only problem is that in a small plane, the already small interior becomes even smaller with these rubberised suits, which although keeping you very warm are extremely uncomfortable. Flying across cold oceans and desolate land, a bright daylight fluorescent orange suit is worn; it is easier to see if you have the misfortune to be paddling in the ocean or lost in the tundra and snow!

We had needed to buy a second immersion suit as I had only brought mine from England. Luckily whilst we were in Florida it just so happened that there was a sale of ex military gear in a market in North Miami. Unluckily the only submersible suit I could find was in rather unbecoming shades of Atlantic Green camouflage. Pretty pointless when you think about it: if we had gone into the water only one of us would have been seen. I tossed a coin into the air and lost, so Denis got to wear my bright `sunglasses required` orange lolly immersion suit, whilst I wore the Atlantic green one. I was obviously feeling very positive that day.

Greenland

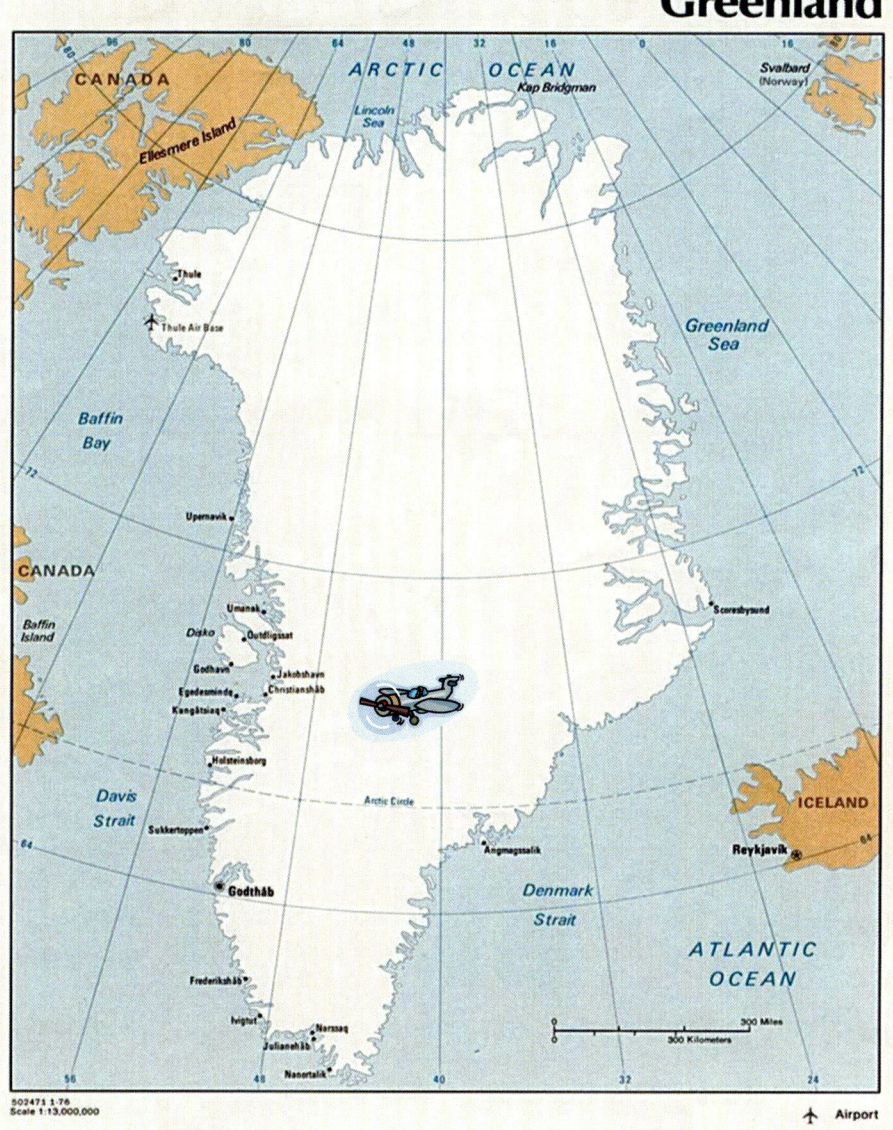

If whilst wearing the costume a need arises to have a wee then good luck! Restricted in movement with several zips and bits of Velcro make this normal task the challenge of the century; maybe a large nappy would be better. Some clever person came up with the apt name of *little John* (or big John for the optimist) for a suitably shaped container for those who were caught short. In addition, there was one for the ladies appropriately named *lady Jane*; again suitably designed. The North Sea oilrig guys and rescue personnel use this type of survival equipment *(the suits, not, I presume, the plastic extras!)*, as do many other people working in harsh environments; consequently the gear has to be good.

A Potentially Wet Hop To Greenland

Encapsulated in our survival suits we resembled two wayward astronauts on our way to a Space Station! I obtained clearance from the Air Traffic Controller, and once more it was up and away leaving Goose Bay en route for Bluie-West-One, Greenland. Parting from the great American continent the Warrior responded to a gentle pull on the control column raising her nose towards the sky. The engine emitted a quiet rumble and the slip stream over the wings a gentle hiss. It was a slow climb due to the weight of our extra food supplies *(mandatory for obvious reasons)*. Looking at the horizon one could see just how isolated Goose Bay was, with only lakes, small wooded areas, hillocks and tundra as far as the horizon. It is around 120 miles up the river to the real Arctic Ocean, and when arriving at the coast, the land disappeared into a mass of rocks of every shape and size, with the sea crashing and foaming all around the inhospitable tributary. The only living beings for miles apart from us in this desolate and forbidding place were the occasional school of whales, and the many sea birds and seals, all vying for the fish that were undoubtedly in the sea.

In the plane, the gremlins started pretty quickly: the main ADF (*Automatic Direction finder*) still had the indicator pointing behind as it had done since leaving Quebec. Not a problem; we carried on using the back up unit, as there would be little point in making a -u-turn. A later investigation in Reykjavik found that some wires had been connected incorrectly when the unit had been repaired. The Loran also started to play up and was working intermittently, so it was down to a stopwatch, map bearings, timed turns, a pencil and a chart – then I lost the pencil sharpener! The course plotted was in part a great circle route and a rhumb line; too short a distance for one and too far for the other. There were four timed heading adjustments on the flight. I wanted the arc to go just north of Narssarssuaq our destination, as the alternative Godhaab was several hundred miles further north by north west. Rather than heading directly for the airport, I followed Sir Francis Chichester's `*off-*

course` doctrine: upon arrival I knew that *a* – I needed to turn right for Narssarssuaq and *b* – I was on the correct side to continue to Godhaab if required.

Sir Francis Chichester, when flying in the pioneering era of the early thirties on his epic voyage across the Ocean from New Zealand to Japan, used the concept of `off-course navigation` *(In off-course navigation you do not correct for wind drift).* You fly the magnetic course you plotted on the map for the length of time calculated it would take to arrive at the destination. Upon arrival you would look `upwind`. For example, if you head directly for the destination and when you `arrive` according to your calculations, you are unable to locate the airstrip, you would not know whether to turn left or right to find the safety of the airport. Amelia Earhart with her navigator may have made that tragic mistake by heading directly for Howland Island to refuel rather than one side of it. When they arrived overhead and could not see land, they perhaps made a turn in the wrong direction robbing the world of two very courageous people.

Further north *(half way up Greenland on the western coast)* was the large American Military Airport of Sondrestrom. There was a very high charge for landing at the military base so it was obviously not worth going that route. The terrain was also higher and with the Warrior's limited maximum altitude the lower southern route through the snow fields and ice plains was a better bet.

Just to throw a spanner in the works, there was the calculation of a `PNR`, the `point of no return` which needed working out. This is based on the fuel available versus the distance, with wind-weather being the variable. At a certain navigational point on my chart I needed to decide if with the wind and weather we could reach the destination airport with a safe margin of fuel. There is little point in continuing past the PNR and running out of fuel and having to land on an ice floe or worse. Therefore, you have to be really certain the weather at your destination is acceptable, and that the runway is clear of any obstruction; if not it would be a 180-degree turn back to Goose Bay.

All aircraft including the big airliners have to complete a PNR calculation with the engine(s) probability factor added in for good measure. A loss of an engine means a decrease in altitude, decrease in speed, a decrease in flyable distance and an increase in fuel consumption. More workload for the pilots and extra strain on the operating engine/s, especially where twin-engine planes are concerned. Therefore the rule is quite clear, loss of an engine on a twin means heading straight to the nearest suitable airport. The four-engine planes with the loss of only one engine have more choice and providing the captain is happy, can continue to the original destination. However, this is not always a good idea and I do not agree with what is effectively a financial decision from the airline. Making an alternate landing is expensive and aircraft operators do not like extra cost even though they already make hundreds of millions of dollars! There is more than one example of serious errors. I remember a large four-engine plane operated by a very well known airline departing from the West Coast of USA, attempting to continue the flight with one engine down traversing America, and then onto an Atlantic crossing. They could not make London and only just made an airport in the north of England. That was dangerous and stupid. The pilot should have been `hauled over the coals` for that serious misjudgement. The American FAA *(Federal Aviation Administration)* fined the airline £20,000, which really was not enough.

As luck would have it some 40 minutes past our PNR the engine sounded a little rough. Although engines cannot differentiate between land and sea, for some unknown reason whenever a single engine plane has water underneath the wings `*hey presto*` the power plant sounds irregular! We were going through some ice cloud and I assumed that we had picked up some engine icing. However when we cleared the cloud, the roughness did not go away. Normally I would have done a magneto check - switching off each of the two magnetos in turn. Thank goodness I did not. Unbeknown to us the main impulse magneto had broken. The primary magneto provides the initial spark impulse for both magnetos and both sets of spark plugs to each cylinder. Had I switched off the main magneto there would have been an eerie silence prior to our demise after being catapulted into the cold Arctic Ocean below. It transpired that although the engine had just been serviced, the magnetos that should have been changed were not, and were in fact the original ones fitted to the engine a good few years previously.

We continued flying on one magneto at a vastly reduced speed of some 82 to 88 MPH instead of 105. Flying in ignorant bliss of the severity of the problem we carried on towards our destination. As I am sure you know, flying to the USA or westward in the northern latitudes normally means there is a fairly strong head wind to contend with, and conversely flying back to Europe a tailwind. On our particular trip the wind was quite fickle, and was only helping at around 10/15 mph. On a previous occasion in a Piper Seneca, I had a tail wind of 70 MPH, which made the trip an awful lot quicker, giving a ground speed of 255 MPH which for a light twin engine airplane was pretty good. It can be quite often the case that a tail or head wind can affect a light aircraft up to 50% of its normal speed. Hence the extreme caution required in planning any trip.

Although Greenland is larger than the UK & western Europe combined, there are only some half dozen airports or airstrips available. As our nearest alternative was 220 miles north of Narssarssuaq, I had to be extremely careful to get a final check of the destination weather via the HF radio. Why it happens to me is a mystery, but even the HF was so crackly *(like a vintage valve radio)* that it was nigh on impossible to hear what anyone was saying. The operation of the radio is not straightforward, and geographical location along with the time of day will determine on which frequency to obtain maximum clarity. The radio waves skip around the planet, with the signal bouncing off the ionosphere. Think of a large beach ball bouncing up and down continuously round the planet and you will get an idea how the signal propagates. If the receiving station happens to be half way between a skip then that is that! I might be able to talk to a radio operator half way round the world, but that does not get me the weather at our destination.

The 121.50 international distress frequency is very useful to call up airliners that are flying much higher, and with line of sight range on VHF, they are much easier to access. So calling out on a normal VHF frequency, I was able to contact a British Airways 747 with crystal clear reception some 28,000 feet above our 9,000 feet cruising level. The pilot confirmed that they were passing southern Greenland and that the co-pilot could see our destination quite clearly even from that altitude. Therefore, with that confirmation of good weather we carried on to Greenland. Most pilots in the big jets are happy to chat to us little guys as it makes a change from their normal routine. Indeed even if they have not flown such a route in a little plane, they would have done their basic flight training in a Piper Warrior or a similar aircraft. The comment often comes back, `*you're flying a what – you are where*`? Memories can often be short - especially when the pilots are flying high and comfortable with

180

the luxury of hot meals and drinks brought into the cockpit when required.

Calling up `sob story` on the radio the North American Strategic Command's Radar Control burst into action and kindly passed on our message and our ETA at Narssarssuaq. The military like to know what is going on in their airspace and always seem friendly and ready to help.

In the most northern and southern latitudes, the lack of pollution and haze offers unparalleled visibility. It was quite something to see the outline of Greenland so crystal clear whilst being over 200 miles away. In the distance, the horizon in front of us was an outline of pure white with peaks sticking out like the teeth of some huge sea monster. I could not look away such was the fascination. Stretching eastwards and northwards, a line of white filled the horizon. So near yet so far in this world of snow and ice.

Even beneath our wings the enthralment and beauty continued. A small group of icebergs of various shapes and sizes like some ice armada was drifting down to meet the Labrador current, and eventually the onslaught of the Atlantic Ocean. A forbidding prospect when in such a small and frail flying machine. As we got closer the contrast was quite distinct, the blue-green waters of the ocean lapping at the foot of the land, and the beautiful deep blue of the sky overhead. Add to that the radiance of the sun, and the view gave us the impression of being in another world.

There have been occasions when in the early days of flying this route, aircrew mistakenly thought that they were much closer than they really were just because of the incredible visibility. These days GPS and DME *(distance measuring equipment)* make the apparent closeness a mere optical illusion, as the instruments will show the aircrew their precise position. In our case I used hands-on dead reckoning, as our navigation system at low level was not working very well. Happily after some 7 hours of flying over nothing but the Arctic Ocean, I started to descend from 9,000 feet over some pack ice towards the southern-most tip of Greenland. Narssarssuaq Control confirmed that with excellent weather, we could continue up the Fjord towards the airport.

Flying a low 1,000 feet on the approach, I looked side to side, as some predator would hunting in a forest. If anything our roles were reversed – me the prey, the cold Arctic Ocean and the polar bear on the ice floe below the hunter. It was a little one sided as white being the colour of the bear and the ice floe, there could have been a hundred bears or only one, I would never have known.

Paradoxically, one really positive point about flying slowly, as opposed to getting there quickly, is that the beauty of the surroundings is revealed, and can be truly enjoyed. At the entrance to the fjord we passed Simiutaq island amid a jumble of rocks. We saw an ancient ramshackle radio station, with its homing beacon aerial rusty and bent over at right angles from the onslaught of wind. This radio station from the Second World War confirmed our position by the needle of the cockpit indicator of the back up unit swinging 180 degrees *(thus indicating that the station was now behind us)*. A further confirmation was our headphones making happy little beeping noises like an excited robotic dog pleased to see its master.

Up the Skovfjord then the Tunugduarfik fjord, remembering that where two fjords meet some 40 miles ahead I must ensure the left hand fork is taken. Having read all I could about Greenland, I learnt that the right hand fork goes into a false entrance and at the end there is only the canyon wall with an old Douglas DC3 embedded in the granite grave. Flying low level it is not possible to turn around, and nor is it possible to climb over the canyon wall unless you are flying a rocket, so the old DC3 would have been the last thing you would see in this world!

However, all was well as I duly turned into the left hand fork. The runway is not visible until another blind turn so my fingers were crossed, but to our relief the little airport came into view exactly where it was supposed to be - happily no sign of a wall of rock! The old folklore of mountain flying came to mind - if the wind speed increases 6 knots or more per 1,000 feet then there is a distinct possibility of wind shear and turbulence on the ground. On the other hand, 20/25 knots of wind on the ground *(around force 5/6 in nautical terms)* would mean quite a turbulent ride over high hills and low mountains, and it is not advisable to fly too close or downwind of these projections. With the close proximity of high mountains each side of the runway, and the chance of a very dangerously strong katabatic wind sliding down off the glacier, caution is the optimum thought of the day. Those condition would have meant more work for my tired brain, but with only a gentle breeze all was well that day.

At the start of the runway there were some small icebergs bobbing about in the water; and moored to a jetty close by was a Danish Fisheries Protection vessel similar to a Royal Navy Frigate. Lining up for the runway which coincidently started at the water's edge, I pushed the nose down whilst easing back on the power, aiming to be just ahead of the ship, which was not an aircraft carrier and no doubt would not be too happy with Denis and I swinging in the rigging. I wanted to touch down on the runway numbers. That way the whole of the runway would be in front of the plane rather than behind. To go around is nigh on impossible due to the close proximity of the mountains - plus with my rough running engine, I would have had insufficient power, so there was but little choice but to land first time. It can be a little hair-raising landing in a strange place, but all went well, and with a gentle squeal of tyres, the little Warrior kissed the runway and once more found herself back on terra firma. It was with relief that I taxied the plane up to the ramp where we were to park for the night.

Welcome To Greenland Hop
`The Flag`

Stopping the Warrior's engine we nigh on fell out of the plane as there is no other way of exiting through the one door wearing survival suits, and surrounded by the life raft and all the other trappings we had on our laps. Especially as we were both clambering for the exit at the same time – talk about rats leaving a sinking ship. Denis fell out onto the wing first, and then tumbled to the ground, with me following close behind. Fortunately, being a remote outpost there was no one around to watch our antics save for one of the ground crew who gave the impression that this sort of thing happens all the time and suggesting that we go to the tower for a coffee. There were only three planes on the ground: an ancient Boeing 727 that had come in from Iceland *(there being just enough runway length to accommodate its size)*, a large bright orange Sikorsky helicopter for the local community *(part passenger and part rescue duties)*, and a small newly launched business Jet Stream turbo prop on its way to Canada.

Narssarssuaq Airport near the base of a glacier (the runway is near bottom left of the photo running up from the water's edge). I took this shot as the plane levelled at 10,000 feet for a normal spiral descent landing over the fjord, when I was making a practice approach after having the engine repaired. You can see the enormous stretch of the glacier when comparing the mountains either side of the runway which go up to 9,000 feet (photo by author).

We needed to stretch our legs after flying 7.7 hours without moving a muscle. Cramp was a problem, and it can get extremely claustrophobic in a little plane, especially accompanied by a 50 gallon drum of aviation fuel.

Truly there were times during the flight when I had felt like opening the door and jumping out, such is the feeling of confinement. However, a refreshing drink and a chat with the Air Traffic Controller made us feel human once again. Still unaware of the crisis with the magneto, and to avoid any condensation building up in the fuel tank overnight, I arranged to refuel the plane immediately ready for an early start in the morning. Normally I would have started the plane and taxied over to the refuelling zone, but even Narssarssuaq had become modernised and the fuel was now delivered to the plane in a small mobile tanker. Fate still had not played her card; at least not knowing about the problem allowed us to have a good night's sleep.

Refuelling in the higher northern or southern latitudes can present its own problems. Mainly because the air is so dry, there can be a dangerous build up of static electricity. When refuelling a plane, helicopter or vehicle, it is absolutely imperative to ensure that the machine is earthed by a cable to the refuelling truck and the ground. For instance, if you started to pour fuel from a large metal can through a plastic funnel thereby breaking the earth line, there is every chance that a spark would be created with a possible fireball destroying the wing and probably the rest of the plane. All aircraft regardless of size have static wicks to discharge electrostatic build-up in the air. You can see them on the rear of the wings of all planes big and small. They are little pieces of plastic tubing with conducting wicks inside protruding into the slipstream. An added problem to contend with is that fuel has a habit of freezing when faced with extreme low temperatures – so I made sure that antifreeze was automatically mixed into the fuel tanks. A frozen fuel pipe is something I could do without!

Some people have asked what happens if lightning hits a plane? It is worth a comment because of the distinct possibility of this happening during flight when there are thunderstorms anywhere up to 100 miles or even more away depending on severity. Michael Faraday became aware of this phenomenon in the mid nineteenth century long before planes were invented. His law, simplified, is as follows: lightning will tear through the air passing through anything that happens to be in its way. Millions of amps and an amazing amount of energy are produced on each strike. A plane ends up being a `Faraday Cage` inasmuch as electric current passes through the line of least resistance i.e .through metal, so will strike the outside of the plane, and then exit through the all important `static wicks`. Damage is normally fairly insignificant, usually a burn mark where the strike was made, or possibly a hole; on occasions though, serious damage can be done. Unfortunately, the intense power in lightning produces a powerful magnetic field similar to a transformer. If this field passes through another electrical conductor i.e. the aeroplane wiring, then a surge of electric current will be induced into that conductor. Therefore, it has been known for much of the aircraft electronics to be seriously damaged *(cooked)* and the basic magnetic compass rendered useless. In our modern age with so many electronics in an aircraft, the designers have their work cut out to develop a plane with as many safety parameters built in as possible.

I believe that in certain circumstances it is possible to have the aura of St. Elmo's fire around the fuselage – similar to the fire around the masts of sailing ships. The spectre of St. Elmo's fire is a bright blue or violet glow, seen during thunderstorms when the ground *(or sea if you are afloat)* is electrically charged. This only happens when there is a high enough voltage in the air between the cloud and the ground/sea and although called a fire it actually isn't - thank goodness!

Hence the main effort goes into weather avoidance. The development and advancement of integrated weather radar and wind shear systems superimposed onto navigational map screens is a giant leap forward. Perhaps the greatest aid to modern airline flying is the fully automated autopilot. So sophisticated that it can, and indeed sometimes does, fly the plane many thousands of miles without any pilot input. In pioneering days, whilst a very basic autopilot was available, many up-and-coming aviation companies would not have them fitted as their comments were, `a pilot is paid to fly not to sit drinking coffee`! These were the good-old *(bad)* days of real lever pulling, knob twirling, and tired pilots.

With no snow forecast for the morning, and the plane safely refuelled. I left the Warrior at the side of the runway, ready for departure; the idea was to do a trial run-up on the ground and a high speed run on the runway to check if there was any lack of power. I was still optimistic that whatever gremlin had slowed us down would have left us by morning.

Leaving the plane, we walked the few metres to the small Arctic Hotel, where the receptionist made us welcome. Standing In the shadows behind her, and looking extremely menacing, there was a giant polar bear towering above us. Fortunately for us but rather less fortunate for the bear, it was stuffed! Standing nearly 9 feet tall in its `bare` feet, *(not that they ever put shoes on)*, even in the afterlife he looked a frightening proposition; my little handgun would have done nothing to such a monster except perhaps to aggravate it. Looking at his extremely long toenails would have made the keenest pedicurist run a mile!

The hotel staff told us that the bear had to be shot as he had wandered off some passing ice floe up to the little settlement, and once there could not be persuaded to leave. Polar bears are a little like humans in that respect, once a steady meal is available - even out of trash bins – the bear sees little point in jumping into ice cold water hunting seals. It can easily knock large garbage containers onto their sides, and then happily rummage through.

It is a sad fact of life that man can screw up big time with the so-called modernisation of *the outer limits* of our fragile civilisation. Explorers often open the way to land which was perfectly ok until the colonisation and exploitation starts. Still I would not be there if it were not for *progress*, so maybe one should keep quiet and concentrate on flying. The hotel staff were very friendly and later we joined a couple of dozen other people for Dinner. This was the first and last time that I tried whale. Both Denis and I agreed that it tasted like fishy pork, and the blubber chunks were awful - tasting like rancid butter. Greenland is allowed by treaty to catch a few certain types of whale, but I doubt if it would be the most popular item on the menu.

Not knowing about our magneto problem we had a peaceful and long overdue sleep. There hadn't been a sound overnight until 8 am when the community helicopter started up for the school run. We got up to a beautiful blue sky, and made our way to the dining room for breakfast. Whilst Neils the helicopter pilot was away dodging icebergs with the school children, we enjoyed the small hotel's own bread and pastries; which were fresh and quite delicious. Filling our plates from the buffet we chatted to the other guests. They were the hardy type of explorer – not a high heel shoe in sight and all talking about - yes you guessed – Greenland. It was a shame to rush away from such an enjoyable scene, but duty called, and we needed to get going whilst the weather was good. If the tail wind turned into a head wind, we simply did not have enough fuel to make Reykjavik with a safe margin.

Completing the pre take-off walk around the plane, I checked the engine carefully and all seemed as it should be. Depending on how complicated a plane is made, there are a few pages to a large manual on checking the various parts of the plane prior to starting the engine(s).

The little Warrior was a simple machine with no retractable undercarriage, cowl flaps, de-icing system etc. and the checks were over in 10 minutes or so. Getting into the cockpit was the usual squeeze, but far more dignified than getting out. I did suggest to Denis that we would have to perfect our method of exit prior to getting back to London.

Once ensconced in our seats I attempted to start the engine. The starter turned the propeller and that was about it! The engine did not attempt to fire up, and I realised that something quite serious had happened to the ignition system, for there was plenty of fuel in the carburettor.

The local "town" of Narsaq – a friendly little settlement with brightly coloured houses in the only green part of Greenland. From the airport, 20 minutes or so by helicopter, or several hours by sea in a local extremely strongly built small ferryboat carrying around 20 persons. In the centre of the picture is the school, no doubt with a crowd of happy children. Can you imagine the snow fights! 8 months of the year, very contented young Greenlanders! (Photo by author taken in the summer with no snow).

There is usually somewhere a guardian angel on standby in case of need, and ours took the form of Neils, a short stocky Dane who we had met the previous evening. Neils flew the large 20-seat helicopter that we saw on the evening we landed, and had heard that morning when he was doing the school run. He arranged for my little plane to be placed in the hangar normally reserved for the helicopter. Being a licensed engineer, he kindly offered to help us in his time off. Later in the day with the engine cowls and the two magnetos removed, he found that the impulse magneto cog that locks into the drive shaft was sheared. It was a shock to both Denis and I and the truth dawned on us just how close we had been to a mid ocean ditching into seriously cold water and ice floes. Luckily, the broken piece of the cog had not fallen into the main part of the engine, and with careful manipulation of a magnet Neils managed to extract it.

The offending magneto that decided to lose a tooth 2 miles above the Arctic Ocean. On the left, the little broken part was found inside the oil filter. (Photo by author).

194

Realising that we were now forced to stay until new parts could be obtained, we checked back into the hotel and surveyed our surroundings. Meanwhile, Neils had got through to the Danish Piper agent in Copenhagen and was arranging for a new unit to be flown out on the next mail plane. He also needed to get an ignition-timing unit, which by a fantastic coincidence was in Sondestrom Airport some 400 miles north of us. An American engineer Neils knew who serviced a couple of light aircraft at the American Air base, had it in his toolbox. It would take a few days to arrive, as we would have to wait until an aircraft was coming this way. Aircraft are the life-support contact in remote locations when there is no other way of getting around; save by ship in the summer months.

The Warrior engine is fired from two magnetos driving the ignition system, which fire up two spark plugs per engine. Yet again Michael Faraday's name comes up: the basic idea was derived from the work he did early in the nineteenth century when he discovered the relationship between electricity and magnetism. Were it not for our early inventors we would probably still be travelling around in horse drawn carriages, and flying would be strictly for the birds.

Whilst waiting for the engine parts, and with time to spare I decided to find out more about Greenland. I discovered that it is the world's largest island, covering 840,000 square miles *(2,175,600 square km)*. It is a dependency of Denmark. The capital is

Nuuk *(Godthåb)* and the island extends about 1,660 miles *(2,670 km)* from north to south and more than 650 miles *(1,050 km)* from east to west at its widest point. Two-thirds of the land mass lies within the Arctic Circle, and the island's northern extremity extends to within less than 500 miles *(800 km)* of the North Pole. At Narssarssuaq we probably were within 2,300 miles of the North Pole, which still seemed a long way away, but looking at the terrain it felt as if we were at the top of the world already. The north west tip of Greenland is separated from Canada's Ellesmere Island by only 16 miles *(26 km)*. But as the whole area is a mass of ice, snow and rocks, the shorter over water distance is not really any use from an aviators point of view.

Although flying direct from Goose Bay to Narssarssuaq is a longer sea route, it is far easier then continuing to fly north as one has to travel considerably further before turning right. No real help for the pilot except there are a couple of airstrips where fuel is available for the plane that has a limited range. The nearest European country is Iceland, across the Denmark Strait. Narssarssuaq is about 700 miles from Iceland, but we were actually intending to go a dogleg route in order to remain near the land as long as possible, in case of further engine problems. Greenland's deeply indented coastline totals 24,430 miles *(39,330 km)*, a distance roughly equivalent to the Earth's circumference at the Equator, and by strange coincidence nearly the same as the coast line of Australia. By contrast the length of the UK coastline is around 11,072 miles *(17,819 km)* which is long compared to the coastline of Italy 7600 km, and Spain 4964 km but absolutely nothing in comparison to Greenland. A `submarine` ridge no deeper than 600 feet *(180 m)* connects Greenland physically with North America, as structurally it is an extension of the Canadian Shield, the rough plateau of the Canadian north that is made up of hard Precambrian rocks. Greenland's major physical feature is its massive ice sheet, which is second only to Antarctica's in size. The ice sheet has an average thickness of 5,000 feet *(1,500 m),* reaches a maximum of about 10,000 feet *(3,000 m),* and covers more than 700,000 square miles, or nearly 85 percent of Greenland's total land area. That is a fair bit of ice when you think it is anything up to 2 miles thick!

It was only about two hours walk from the airport to the start of the immense glacier, which looked as if some huge giant *(or superman)* had frozen the flow of water in midstream. Denis and I walked across the extremely wide shallow gravel bed, hopping on the odd boulder to keep from getting wet, and were rewarded when we came up to the glacier. The sight was breathtaking and awesome. Over the centuries layers of snow falling on the barren windswept surface became compressed into ice layers, which constantly move outward to the peripheral glaciers.

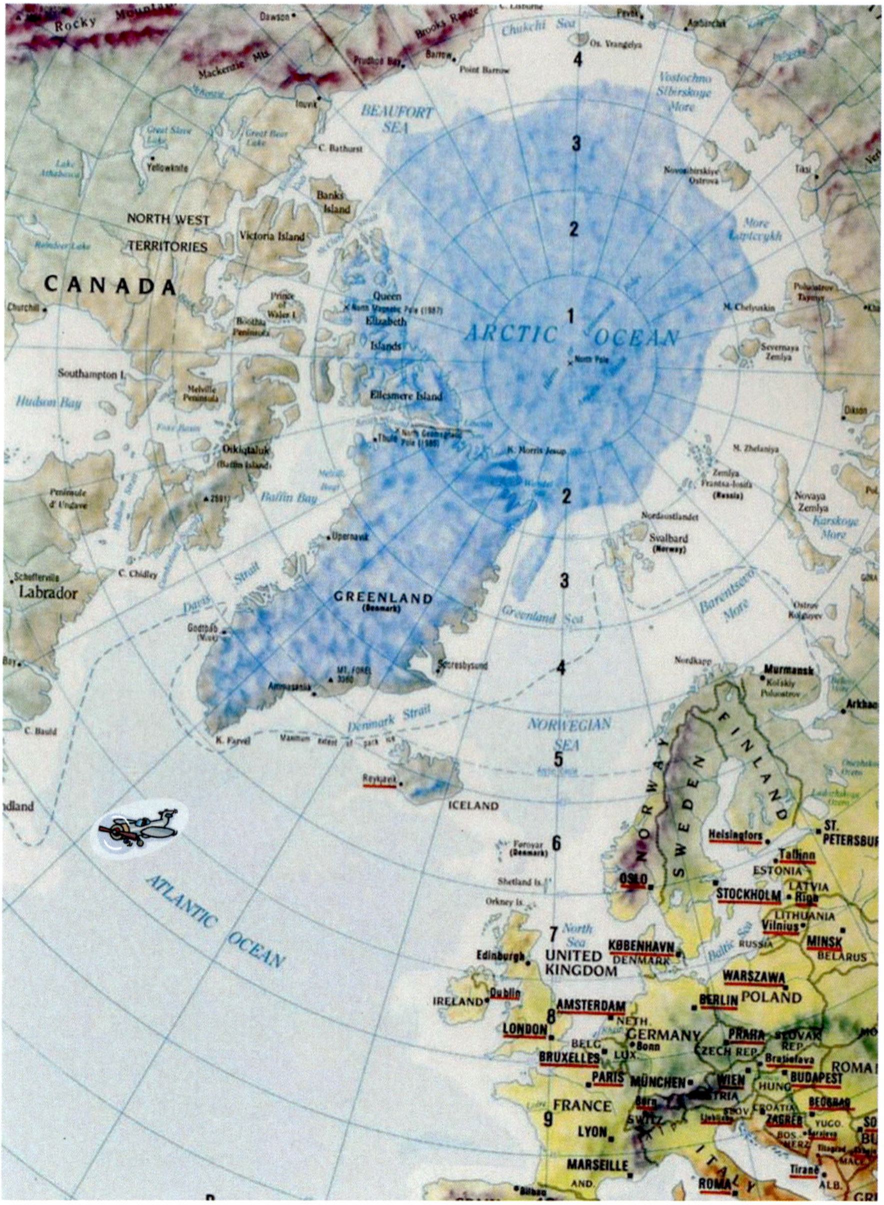
Dawson
Brooks Range
Chukchi Sea
Os. Vrangelya
Pevek
Ambarchik
Mackenzie Mts.
Prudhoe Bay
Barrow
Point Barrow
Inuvik
BEAUFORT SEA
Vostochno Sibirskoye More
Great Slave Lake
Great Bear Lake
Yellowknife
Lake Athabasca
C. Bathurst
Banks Island
Novosibirskiye Ostrova
Tiksi
NORTH WEST TERRITORIES
Victoria Island
More Laptevykh
Reindeer Lake
CANADA
Prince of Wales I.
Queen Elizabeth Islands
North Magnetic Pole (1987)
Boothia Peninsula
Churchill
ARCTIC OCEAN
M. Chelyuskin
Poluostrov Taymyr
North Pole
Severnaya Zemlya
Southampton I.
Melville Peninsula
Hudson Bay
Ellesmere Island
Dikson
Foxe Basin
Thule
North Geomagnetic Pole (1986)
K. Morris Jesup
M. Zhelaniya
Qikiqtaaluk (Baffin Island)
Zemlya Frantsa-Iosifa (Russia)
Peninsule d' Ungave
Baffin Bay
Novaya Zemlya
Karskoye More
Nordaustlandet
Svalbard (Norway)
Upernavik
Schefferville
Labrador
C. Chidley
Davis Strait
GREENLAND (Denmark)
Greenland Sea
Barentsevo More
Ostrov Kolguyev
Godthåb (Nuuk)
Nordkapp
Murmansk
Kolskiy Poluostrov
Scoresbysund
Mt. Forel 3360
Ammassalik
Denmark Strait
NORWEGIAN SEA
C. Bauld
K. Farvel
Maximum extent of pack ice
FINLAND
NORWAY
SWEDEN
Reykjavik
ICELAND
Helsingfors
Tallinn
ESTONIA
Føroyar (Denmark)
OSLO
STOCKHOLM
LATVIA
Riga
Shetland Is.
Orkney Is.
LITHUANIA
Vilnius
MINSK
ATLANTIC OCEAN
North Sea
Edinburgh
UNITED KINGDOM
KØBENHAVN
DENMARK
RUSSIA
BELARUS
Baltic Sea
WARSZAWA
IRELAND
Dublin
AMSTERDAM
BERLIN
POLAND
NETH.
LONDON
GERMANY
Bonn
PRAHA
SLOVAK REP.
BELG.
BRUXELLES
LUX.
CZECH REP.
Bratislava
PARIS
MÜNCHEN
WIEN
BUDAPEST
HUNG.
AUSTRIA
Bern
FRANCE
SWITZ.
CROATIA
ZAGREB
BEOGRAD
YUGO.
LYON
ITALY
BOS.-HERZ.
Sarajevo
MARSEILLE
Tiranë
ROMA
ALB.
AND.
Bilbao
4
3
2
1
2
3
4
5
6
7
8
9

The Jakobshavn Glacier, often moving 100 feet *(30 meters)* a day, is among the world's fastest glaciers. The remaining small part of ice-free *(but not snow free)* land occupies the country's coastal areas and consists largely of highlands. Mountain chains parallel the island's east and west coasts, rising to 12,139 feet *(3,700 m)* at Gunnbjørns Fjeld in the southeast. These highlands notwithstanding, most parts of the rock floor underlying Greenland's ice sheet are in fact at, or slightly beneath, current sea levels. Long, deep fjords reach far into the east and west coasts of Greenland in complex systems, offering magnificent, if desolate, scenery. Along many parts of the coast, the ice sheet fronts directly onto the sea, with large chunks breaking off and sliding into the water as icebergs. The problem for the increasing numbers of modern tourists who want to visit the harder-to-get-to places, is access.

Apart from the very well equipped and experienced explorer with expensive back up, 99% of Greenland is inaccessible. Tourists usually get flown by helicopter to the Glacier top so they are able to take a short walk on it. Flying a small plane or a helicopter is still the best way of seeing this magnificent island. Greenland is actually larger than Western Europe and with only some 60,000 inhabitants, it can be a very lonely place. But even this magnificent land of ice, snow and mountains can get monotonous with its perpetual white landscape, and beautiful as it is, I began to long for the green hills of England.

The climate of Greenland is bleak and arctic, modified only by the slight influence of the Gulf Stream in the southwest; hence the strategic position there of Narssarssuaq. Rapid weather changes, from sunshine to impenetrable blizzards, are common and result from the eastward progression of low-pressure air masses over a permanent layer of cold air above the island's icy interior. (*Yet another reason to check on the weather at* Narssarssuaq *prior to departing*). The average winter *(January)* temperatures range from 21 F *(-6 C)* in the south to -31 F *(-35 C)* in the north. A vast change, but considering the length of Greenland it becomes more understandable.

Having previously experienced a week of arctic winter in Anchorage, Alaska, I can readily testify to just how cold minus 30 centigrade is, and how the survival situation can change literally overnight into something approaching dangerous. Summer temperatures along the southwestern coast average 45 F *(7 C)* during July though this has risen considerably over the years due to global warming. The average summer temperature in the far north is 39 F *(3.6 C)*.

The average annual precipitation decreases from more than 75 inches (1,900 mm) in the south to about 2 inches (50 mm) in the north. However, such was the daytime warmth of the sun in the microclimate of southwest Greenland, it was comparable to the Mediterranean, and we were walking around in tee shirts - admittedly with goose pimples! However it becomes extremely cold when the sun goes down, and we needed our fleece lined jackets.

A low aerial view flying up a fjord 500 feet above the ice floes (not a place for an engine breakdown).
(Photo by author).

The country's vegetation is characterized mainly as tundra and consists of such plants as sedge, cotton grass, and lichen; the limited ice-free areas are almost totally devoid of trees, although some dwarfed birch, willow, and alder scrub do manage to survive. Seven species of land mammals: polar bears, musk oxen, reindeer, arctic foxes, snow hares, ermines, and lemmings can be found on the island. Though I have to say that the only non human I saw was the polar bear in the hotel and he was stuffed! Seals and whales abound in the chilly waters and were formerly the chief source of nourishment for the Greenlanders. Cod, salmon, flounder and halibut are important saltwater fish, and the island's rivers contain salmon and trout.

Despite the western influence exerted by the Danish presence in Greenland, many of the island's people continue to practice traditional Inuit cultural activities. Folk arts, especially soapstone carving and drum dancing, remain popular. In 982 the Norwegian Erik the Red, who had been banished from Iceland for manslaughter, settled in Greenland. Returning to Iceland in 985, he referred to the newly discovered land as Greenland in order to make people more willing to go there. In 986 he organized an expedition back to Greenland, which resulted in the development of two main settlements: the East Settlement, near present-day Julianehåb, and the West Settlement, near present-day Nuuk.

These settlements may have reached a maximum population of 3,000 on 280 farms. Christianity arrived in the 11th century by way of Leif Eriksson, who had just returned from the recently Christianized Norway. A bishop's seat was established in Greenland in 1126. Beginning sometime in the 13th century, the Norse *(Norwegian)* settlers began to interact with the expanding Inuit Thule culture that had appeared in northern Greenland about 1100 AD. Norse Greenland had been a republic until 1261, when the colonists swore allegiance to the King of Norway. The Norse settlements declined in the 14th Century however, mainly because of a cooling in Greenland's climate, and in the 15th century they became extinct.

After the disappearance of the original Norse settlements, no attempt at colonization was made until 1721, when Hans Egede, with the permission of the united kingdom of Denmark-Norway, founded a trading company and Lutheran mission near present-day Godthåb; thus marking the real beginning of Greenland's colonial era. In 1776 the Danish government assumed full monopoly of trade with Greenland, and the Greenland coast was closed to foreign access until 1950. What happened during this long period of isolation is a little unclear, though it is known Denmark did try to gradually acclimatize the Greenlanders to the outside world whilst avoiding the danger of economic exploitation. I find that strange considering how few ships would have made such perilous voyages in the 17th and 18th Century.

Greenland fell under the protection of the United States during the German occupation of Denmark *(1940-45)* and was returned to Denmark in 1945. Following the war, Denmark responded to the Greenlanders' complaints over its administration of the island. The Greenlanders are principally of Inuit, or Eskimo, extraction, but they are very strongly admixed with early European immigrant strains.

A view from 12,000 feet leaving south west Greenland heading north east for the ice fields and glaciers. In the distance the snow fields can be seen, and the fjords make way for the uncharted interior (photo by author).

The monopoly of the Royal Greenland Trading Company was abolished in 1951, and after Greenland became an integral part of the Kingdom of Denmark in 1953, reforms were undertaken to improve the local economy, transportation, and education. Home rule was not achieved until May 1,

1979. Pop. (*1991 est.*) 56,500. More than four-fifths of the population are native Greenlanders; about one-sixth are immigrant Danes.

In the 1980s pure Inuit were found only in the extreme northwest, around Thule, and in the east. The population of Greenland is widely dispersed, mostly in very small coastal settlements, and I imagine from my short experience that it can be a very lonely place for its inhabitants. The country's principal exports, zinc and lead are the main ores mined. The other products are frozen, tinned, dried, and smoked fish; as well as processed mineral-ore concentrates. Greenland's chief trading partners are Denmark, Norway, Germany, and the United States. The island receives financial aid from Denmark.

Roadways in Greenland are limited to short stretches of ice-free coastal areas. I saw perhaps 1 mile of road, the rest were gravel tracks. Dog sledges are used inland along with the ever present noisy motorised sledges. Shipping and air service are the principal means of transport. The Island has sophisticated tele-communications installed, as well as a military communications network associated with NATO and the North American radar defence system. The internet and other electronic goodies which are now readily available to the inhabitants seem so out of place in this distant and remote ice world of Greenland – or am I being selfish?

It is a fantastic and interesting land well worth visiting. With all this talk about global warming, even if it is exaggerated, the Greenland that I knew could well be a thing of the past. After all, the north pole is only ice and snow surrounded by land. What a different picture would present itself with those two essential items no longer with us. At least Antarctica would still be there. I can imagine tour operators re-writing maps and showing it as a beautiful beach resort with large mountain ranges.

I was interested to know that close by Narssarssuaq airport on a gravel bed there is a large old building erected by the Americans during the Second World War and enlarged afterwards. It was originally a hospital and supply base and then probably used for injured American soldiers from the Korean War, and was situated in this remote place to avoid the prying eyes of the Press and, no doubt, the public. Who knows with the progress of today, some enterprising person may attempt a rapid conversion into a luxury hotel. What a tragedy if that were to happen; Greenland needs to remain bleak and beautiful, and perhaps a little aloof from the rest of our commercial world?

A (delayed) Local Test Flight Hop

Back to working on the plane, and with the new magneto in place it was time to see if the little Warrior would start. Sitting in the seat like an excited school boy, switching on the master circuit, I primed the engine and turned the key. The propeller swung one way and then the other and then a large backfire sound came out of the engine exhaust with a puff of smoke. Oh what now? A few hours later, after removing the starter motor, a crack revealed itself across the gear pinion that locates into the engine flywheel.

Difficult to see – but the drive cog of the starter had split along the raised part of the gear. (Photo by author).

This was another unexpected delay, not to mention the cost. There seemed no reason why this should have happened. Neils put it down to excessive fuel in the engine when being primed causing a late detonation of the spark, which caused the backfire. So, another frantic call to the Piper dealer in Copenhagen, who managed to find a starter on the shelf and promised to get it flown out in a couple of days on the next mail plane. We made a few frantic calls to England via satellite at a cost that defied belief to assure that all was well, but that there would be a few days delay. Unfortunately we learned that the news was not good, Denis had lost an important job, and I in turn had some problems with my Company.

It all seemed a little unreal: we were on the world's largest island, the least populated place on our planet, surrounded by the Arctic Ocean plus icebergs and with a colossal glacier a couple of hours walk away. One wonders why we bothered to make the calls. Our dream could have lasted longer.

Attempting to forget work problems, we joined Neils in the helicopter with other passengers and freight on a sightseeing tour to the village of Narsaq. Some 40 minutes later, we arrived at a gaily-decorated hamlet complete with a small eating-house and school. No cars, just motor snow bikes, sledges, and the odd tractor. The weather was perfect and apart from some icebergs in the small harbour the snow had retreated a long way back into the foothills. It was such a peaceful place, with friendly people

Denis and I were feeling more than a bit peckish, so we presented ourselves at the little combined shop & café. Neither of us could speak the language properly, but I made some passable sentences, thanks to my brother who by marrying a Danish girl some years ago, gave me the incentive to learn a very limited amount of the language..

A posed photo in the sun of Neils in his day-glow orange suit repairing the engine, and myself. Narssarssuaq, Greenland (photo by Denis).

Denis had this amazing way with people, and by smiling cheerfully, gesturing with his hands, and making various appropriate sounds, they immediately understood that we wanted a substantial meal. I think he could have convinced a polar bear that we were hungry! He really should have been a mime actor. Although the food served was basic, it was certainly sufficient for 2 hungry explorers. You can imagine the menu? Fish and chips and yet more fish! However we knew that the Greenlandic folk actually have quite a choice of food; there are hardy beef cattle and sheep on the island to supplement the fish diet. In fact because they make their own bread and cakes there is no real need for outside influence. But unfortunately children being children, there are imported goodies selling at vastly inflated prices in the one and only shop. Packets of crisps, cans of drink, chocolate and all the junk food with which we tempt the young ones were readily available.

In the harbour there was a ferry that had the look of a small icebreaker. The jovial skipper, complete with red beard *(bearing a slight resemblance to Eric the Red),* was taking some Inuit to their remote homesteads and then onto the airport. In an ever-adventurous mood, we hitched a ride. The trip would take 4 hours allowing for an erratic route to avoid the icebergs as the boat weaved its way out to sea.

Although English was not widely spoken, you can just see Denis *(top left head)* striking up a conversation with our fellow passengers. Tourists were not commonplace and we were all interested in learning about each other. One passenger, a

210

native Greenlander, was getting ready to depart for Germany and thence to University. Her English was understandable, and proud of her Inuit background, she told us a lot about the culture that made up this hardy race. Equally interesting was the invitation to a small farewell party for our newfound friend at one of the flats by the airport. That evening when we arrived the old custom of rubbing noses as a greeting was still used – leastways, it was at this particular function! A very pleasant evening with 10 or so Danish and Greenlandic people, all having a great time along with two English flyers. It certainly made us forget about the engine problems, and work problems back in England. Being in a warm flat with modern music blaring out of the Hi-Fi it all seemed quite surreal.

It was not until well after midnight, when we stepped out into the cold with the icebergs glistening in the moonlight a few metres from our path, that the journey we were undertaking suddenly hit us. What a task we had set ourselves! Passing a couple of snowmobiles, *(which look like motor scooters with a large belt instead of wheels),* really brought home to us that London, and what we questionably call civilisation, was still a long way away. The world suddenly seemed rather large, and relying on a broken down little single engine plane to get us home was quite scary. Meanwhile our pathway was lit by the stars in a sparkling array of dots, and was bright enough for us to find our little hotel some 500 metres from the flat. Apart from the slowly fading music, there was not a sound – just the absolute peace and tranquility which seems to go hand in hand with the icy wastelands of the Arctic.

Polar bear was waiting for us in the hotel reception, looking quite eerie in the subdued light of the night. Both Denis and I were pretty tired so we said goodnight and headed for our respective beds. At least we did not need to find our keys as rooms were never locked.

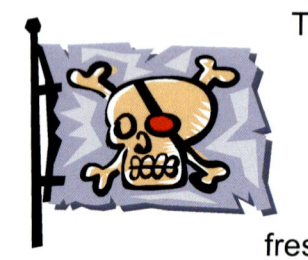

The following day our VIP status seemed to stay with us. First the party invitation, and then after breakfast we were invited aboard the Danish Fisheries vessel for morning coffee and fresh Danish patisseries. We were a little concerned as we hadn`t anything even vaguely smart to wear, but luckily we found everyone was dressed in casual gear. Even the Captain had on a white polar neck pullover instead of his normal uniform. It was a little reminiscent of the old war movies where the captain of the ship, standing on the open bridge and fighting against the odds with dive-bombers and submarines all around, still looked miraculously clean in his white jumper.

Apparently there was an ulterior motive from the Captain's point of view - to practice his English on two marooned Englishmen! However it was a very pleasant and informative couple of hours. Denmark has a reputation for great patisseries, and I have to

212

say that the ones we ate were the best ever. Drinking our coffee and looking out from the bridge at a small iceberg drifting towards us, I couldn't help thinking it was a little too close, but as no one seemed perturbed, we carried on our conversation about sea exploration. Down in the depths of the ship we were shown the small laboratory where a marine biologist could store and examine the various sea creatures extracted from the deep; creatures I had never seen or heard of before.

The author in Narsaq harbour. There was a time when there was more ice than sea – global warming has changed all that! (photo by Denis).

Sadly the time came for us to take our leave, and bidding farewell to the Captain and crew, we departed clutching little bags of cakes and other goodies to eat on our flight home. I could not help thinking about Peter Pan and Captain Hook as we walked down the rickety gangplank off the ship, hoping that there were no big crocodiles in the sea, should we have the misfortune to slip. As we left, the ship was preparing to set sail back into the Arctic Ocean and patrol the seas doing whatever Fisheries Protection ships do for a living. The Danish are keen to be seen taking care of Greenland and keeping the local inhabitants happy. Fishing is their way of life and the Greenlandic people most certainly do not want large foreign factory fishing ships depleting their stocks.

The Navy also keeps an eye on the whales; and no doubt there are scientific people who need a regular input of data from the `men on the spot`. Beluga whales are entirely arctic and sub arctic. They inhabit the Arctic Ocean and its adjoining seas, including the Bering and Beaufort Seas, Baffin Bay and Hudson Bay. During the summer months most belugas inhabit waters where temperatures may be as low as 0-C *(32-Fahrenheit)*. They swim among the icebergs and ice floes of south west Greenland. Belugas are generally found in shallow coastal waters, and we often looked out of the plane trying to catch a glimpse of these strange white creatures but to no avail. Though I have to say when leaving Greenland for Iceland, I did see some `lumps` in the sea which could well have been the elusive Beluga.

Later that day after having had a good walk to counter the effect of eating too many cakes, we decided to give the plane a good polish in anticipation of our homeward journey. In the evening, our little hotel was quite busy and we spent an enjoyable end of day meal with Neils and some of his friends. We watched the arrival of a group of specialist scientists investigating glacial movements; that sounds like it will be long drawn out affair! No doubt Neils and his helicopter would be called upon to drop them on the ice cap.

Getting up next day to a bright sunny morning there was good news. The mail plane had landed and we were told that our spare part had arrived, and to put icing on the cake, Neils had the morning off from flying his helicopter. So apart from any distress calls which would have meant him rushing off, the morning was ours. With a few groans, grunts and words in Danish that we could only guess the meaning of, the new starter was fitted. Neils spoke excellent English, except when he was quietly saying something whilst working in the confines of the engine compartment!

With the new part in place, I attempted to start the engine, but it repeated exactly what had happened three days previously. `*This cannot be happening*` I said to myself. The propeller swung one way and the other, and a large backfire sound came out of the engine exhaust with a puff of smoke. Once again Neils removed the offending starter, which had developed a crack in a similar place to the last one.

He could not understand how this could have happened and so rechecked all his work. After much delving into workshop manuals, it appears that he had inadvertently wired the timing mechanism of the magneto 180 degrees out of alignment. Evidently something that can easily happen as the instructions were not very clear.

It was not feasible to wait for yet another starter, apart from the cost, so we decided to hand start the engine by swinging the propeller. Hand starting was the old fashioned way, at which Denis happened to be an expert, having owned a very old Auster which had no electrics whatsoever. Neils re-adjusted the timing to the correct position, and away went the engine on the third swing. As it was getting towards mid afternoon before we had finished assembling the engine covers (*Neils having disappeared up the coast in his bright orange helicopter delivering some equipment),* we decided to spend the rest of the day relaxing over more coffee and patisseries, and head off the next day to Reykjavik.

Morning came along welcoming us to a beautiful blue sky, the mountain tops a brilliant contrast of white, and the sun a radiant ball of yellow reflecting off the odd lump of ice floating in the harbour. Good omens for a test flight, and with a certain amount of trepidation I taxied the plane to the runway, having left Denis on the ground just in case of any problems. Receiving clearance to take off, I pointed the nose down the centre line and left the ground passing in front of the jetty where the Fisheries ship had been moored the previous day. Initially I went up the western side of Greenland and flew over some small land-bound seas with an assortment of icebergs scattered all over the surface, revealing an endless beauty in a savage desolate sort of way – most certainly not the place to have a mechanical failure. Increasing the power and pointing the nose heavenwards, I climbed up to 10,000 feet heading north in a large orbit, and was rewarded by a most spectacular view of southern Greenland. As far as the eye could see *(and the visibility was without end)* there was a vista of pure white stretching northwards for a thousand miles and more. Fortunately, no problems occurred with the engine, and after a couple of hours flying along what can only be described as one of the most beautiful and isolated coastlines in the world, I dropped a wing and turned back to the airfield. On landing I was greeted by smiles from Denis and Neils who were obviously pleased to see me return in one piece.

As mentioned earlier airports near large mountains occasionally have severe turbulence due to downdrafts. Narssarssuaq has the added problem of a huge glacier ending some 8 miles from the runway. With a combination of strong winds and large temperature differences it is possible to have a katabatic wind in excess of 80 miles per hour funneling down between the mountains. Conversely there could have been an anabatic wind going the other way – which can be just as unpleasant; but happily the winds were benign during our stay. Many of the outlying areas in the world have various folklores, often concerning weather. True or false, it is a wise person who listens and does not scorn such tales. Unfortunately these words of wisdom are only available locally – it could sometimes be helpful to have foreknowledge!

Weather To Go, Or *Whether* Not To Go, Greenland To Iceland Hop

Because ferry flying can be quite a dangerous affair, time consuming and badly paid, this was to be one of my last long haul trips. As it happened I had been offered part time air charter work in Europe, which would keep me out of mischief. However, I would have given anything to have flown the whole of Greenland northwards, as I really wanted to attempt to fly to the North Pole. Unfortunately, without mammoth financial back up it was not possible. The main problem is that towards the top of Greenland and beyond there is nowhere to obtain fuel and the 800 mile range we had in the Piper Warrior was not enough – not enough to reach the top of the world, let alone get back! Obtaining permission was also fraught with problems – maybe another time, who knows!

Another 720 odd miles to go to civilization – well Iceland does have a little bit more than Greenland in the way of people, shops, and restaurants! Difficult to explain unless you have actually been to Greenland, but the land mass that makes up this unique island seems to hold you like some magnetic charm. People who live there have no real urge to see the modern world as we know it – they live close to nature - almost becoming part of that land of snow and ice.

It was a nostalgic departure from Narssarssuaq. Only by leaving do you become aware of just how lovely and unique this part of the world is, and I hope it will stay that way. Narssarssuaq`s geographic position is approximately 61.10 degrees north and 45.50 west and the intention was to fly further north over part of the Greenland ice cap before turning towards Iceland. We prepared to board the Warrior, said our goodbyes to new found friends *(not forgetting the polar bear),* and a very big thank you to Neils, who had so kindly helped us in our moments of difficulty. I must give special mention here to the SAS *(Scandinavian Air Services)* who let us use the hanger for our repairs; and to each of the few but very helpful staff at the airport.

This forced stopover taught me that sometimes I *(along with many others)* tend to rush life, and perhaps it would be better to slow down and enjoy places instead of being ever ready to say `Time to go`. We left late afternoon and because we were flying east, we were in fact `chasing night`. Taking off at 5.30 pm, at our destination it was already 8.30 pm. We had between 7 and 8 hours of flying to do, so my estimate for Reykjavik was around 4 o'clock local time the following morning. Although you are travelling into a later time you are in fact flying into a new day.

Crossing Greenland over the snow fields with the mountains in the distance, words cannot describe the sensation which is quite surreal. In fact below the wing, the white expanse looks like cloud – hence the necessity to always fly on instruments otherwise you can become a flying plough! (Photo from the Piper Warrior by the author).

Lining up on the runway and with our onward clearance confirmed by Air Traffic Control, we took off initially to the west. Climbing steadily, albeit slowly, in a series of large circles over the fjord, we made our way above the mountain ranges and turning towards the east levelled off at 9,000 feet.

A certain Mish Delinger once described the Aurora Borealis, which is so often found in this part of the world:

"Far north in the night sky, a faint glow appears on the horizon. Green and red flames of light stretch across the sky. A glowing curtain of light forms, waving and swirling above you. As the lights fade away the dark night closes over you once again".

In the summer with the sun barely setting, bright stars or flashing lights were unfortunately not `*on the menu*` for this flight. Nevertheless we were rewarded with the beautiful spectacle of a `*double sun*`. The sun setting in the west, only to reappear moments later in the east, is something very special to behold. Somen of the mountains were higher than we were flying and distant snow made the horizon blend into the skyline. Vertigo and spatial disorientation were very real hazards.

Ice floes in the Arctic Ocean as far as the eye can see. One big lump in the bottom of the picture was enormous in comparison with all the small floes. (Photo by the author).

A good few years ago during the 2nd world war, a Catalina twin engine amphibious sea plane on a ferry flight was flying in a snowstorm and as such had little reference to anything outside the plane. Going from west to east across the snowfields of Greenland the crew suddenly felt a gigantic jolt. The engines had stopped and in the scary silence there was no sensation of the plane falling out of the sky – everything had just stopped moving. When the crew unfuddled their fuddled minds, they realised that they must have slowly descended and flown into a giant snowdrift! This can happen if there is a large pressure change and/or one of the outside sensor tubes gets blocked giving an incorrect reading to the altimeter. They were not rescued for quite a few weeks and were very lucky to have survived the long and extremely cold wait. Fortunately as the plane itself was a rescue plane there was plenty of food supplies on board. This is just one of the many true stories of amazing flying incidents over Greenland.

The Catalina was originally designed to be a patrol bomber, an aircraft with a long operational range intended to locate and attack enemy transport ships at sea, in order to compromise the adversary's supply lines. It was also used with great success as a rescue plane to pick up downed crews in the oceans. With a mind to a potential conflict in the Pacific Ocean, where troops would require re-supply over great distances, the US Navy in the 1930`s invested millions of dollars in developing long-range flying boats for this purpose. They were also used to a lesser degree in the North Atlantic. The strange thing about this incident is why was it flying over the ice cap, when the sea would have been a far better medium; bearing in mind that it was a seaplane? The endurance was over 1,500 miles, so Goose Bay to

Iceland in one hop flying south of Greenland was quite feasible. Flying boats had the advantage of not requiring land and in effect have the entire ocean available as a runway. The Navy adopted several different flying boats, but the PBY Catalina was the most widely used.

The impression from looking out of our cockpit window was one of total serenity and beauty; apart from the engine noise it was if the plane was standing still. We were lulled into a sense of peace, and were happy in a rather worrying way. A false sense of security seemed to overpower us and we could easily have fallen asleep, which would have been the end of us. Perhaps the soothing music that was plugged into the intercom system was a little too soothing!

A short extract from my *Polar Navigation* study book tells all. Visibility is usually excellent when there are no interfering clouds or ice crystals haze. However, when snow obliterates surface features, and the sky is covered with a uniform layer of cirrostratus or altostratus clouds, so that there are no shadows, the horizon disappears and the earth and sky blend together, forming an unbroken expanse of white, without features. Landmarks cannot be distinguished, and with complete lack of contrast, distance and height above ground are virtually impossible to estimate. Fortunately, on this flight, there was little cloud but I still had to be careful, bearing in mind that many of the mountains were higher than us. The Piper Warrior could not maintain the higher altitudes of the Piper Seneca or the Cessna 336/337 and it was quite difficult to judge some of the mountain tops. The view over the ice cap was dreamlike and it made us feel quite humble to be an integral part of our planet even if we were cocooned in a metal machine.

A previous trip I did in a twin engine Piper Seneca was not in such good weather conditions – and that was no fun! Doing 200 plus miles an hour with the vastness of space all around, without even seeing the nose of the aircraft, can be quite alarming at times. When I had looked out of the windscreen everything was white, above, below, in front, either side, and even behind there was nothing to see. Only the deadened roar of the two engines running in harmony, a gentle vibration, and the instruments in the cockpit indicated that I was not in a white painted cell, but in a flying machine in cloud above the Greenland ice cap. I had quickly focused my eyes on the flight instruments, lest I became a victim of spatial disorientation, which would result in a rapid spin and final termination of the flight.

With no flight attendants in the little Piper Warrior to bring us coffee and lunch, Denis and I opened our `food parcel` which consisted of a warm flask of drink, some sandwiches, and a few bars of chocolate. However, with the sun shining through the cockpit window and a spectacular view unfolding beneath the wings we would have been happy nibbling on crusts!

Leaving east Greenland for Iceland with solid pack ice in the distance up to the shoreline (photo by the author).

Listening through the headphones to music by Pink Floyd, and Jean Mitchell Jarre playing Oxygen, helped to make this journey across the ice cap even more dreamlike. These musicians may not be so well known now, but in their day it was a new sound, and experimentation with the extremes of music. Apart from which, I believe Jean Mitchell Jarre was the first western group to play in both Russia *(arguably the best music concert ever held)* and China – so he had to be something special.

Flying up the eastern side of Greenland before turning towards Iceland, the land broke into the sea with a continuous assortment of rocks. It was as if a giant had used a large cheese grater and ground the edges of Greenland into shreds of stone. There were numerous rock-strewn inlets where the sea tumbled over itself as if anxious to make passage into the hinterland. At the latitude of 62.50 north above a place called Tingniamuit Fjord, I turned right towards Iceland, and going over a little island called Uvtorsiutit we left Greenland.

Looking back over the military navigational maps probably 90 percent of the places in Greenland are un-pronounceable other than by the locals; with the other 10 percent pronounced incorrectly. The maps had some of the best detail of any maps in the world regarding the rugged contours of the coastline, but the rest was coloured white, not because of the snow but because white was the standard colour for the unknown. Our knowledge of the moon is greater than our knowledge of the icy wastes of Greenland.

Way above the broken ice pack and into open waters we were rewarded by the sight of a school of whales gracefully and majestically making their way north. As we passed over the Denmark Straits it brought back the stories of the Second World War and the hunt for the massive German battle cruiser the Bismarck. The seas looked so inhospitable, and one can only imagine on a dark winter's evening with a storm blowing, how it must have been for the sailors of the hunters and the hunted. They would be using high pressure steam hoses to wash the ice off the deck and superstructure; otherwise the ship could capsize with so much weight on top. The ice was part seawater and part heavy rain, freezing like a super cooled monster onto the ships` metal frames. The conditions defied belief and anyone unfortunate enough to fall overboard would never have been seen again. On top of all the other dangers the ships would have had to have good `*look-outs*` watching for the pack ice, which even in summer is quite extensive.

Our journey was progressing well and we had first-class radio contact with `*Sob Story*`, our American friends, plus the odd plane at a higher altitude that then relayed our messages to Iceland. As an offset heading indicator, I was also listening to music from a long range medium wave radio station in land locked Switzerland. Taking bearings and plotting the course on the chart confirmed our approximate position. In fact, later, when leaving Iceland heading towards Scotland, tuning in to Radio 4 or the World Service can also give a rough heading. That is assuming that you know the position of the transmitting aerial. In the depths of my flight bag, I had a useful little book which gave a list of every radio station in the world, the transmitter location, the latitude and longitude and the listening frequency.

The sun setting over the Denmark Straits, with Greenland behind, and the warmth of Reykjavik beckoning us onwards. It is just possible to see the red tinges of the sun flaring upwards spreading out left and right like a fan in the formation of an Aurora Borealis (photo by the author).

As I mentioned, it is a strange phenomenon to watch the sun disappearing on the port wing, and a little while later see it rising up on the right. It gives the feeling that one has just flown around the world in a couple of hours. Suddenly the twilight of night is transformed into early morning. It was around 4 am when we arrived over Reykjavik Harbour. The Air Traffic Controller gave us a straight-in approach with the Instrument Landing System guiding me down to the start of the runway. Reykjavik was lit in a blazing glory of colour like a massive Christmas tree. With the airport being situated close to the town centre, there were so many lights that it would have been nigh on impossible to have safely made a dawn landing without navigation aids. After some 7 hours of flight tiredness played a part, and to make things worse, the rising dawn sun was glaring into my eyes as I landed into the east.

Once again we were plagued by technical problems - a flickering alternator light illuminated the cockpit in an orange glow as I did a close-down check. We agreed to leave that problem until later; there was only so much a tired brain can assimilate, and without any delay from Customs and very little paperwork, we were cleared to the Arctic hotel *(a great place and well used by pilots),* which was just a few minutes' walk away. We were looking forward to getting a peaceful sleep and pleased that we had escaped the constant droning of the Warrior's engine.

A long lie in was the order of the day, so breakfast was a late affair, more like lunch; our biological clocks still confused as to what time it actually was. In reality being in Iceland made us realise that the prospect of getting home was suddenly very real. Mid afternoon I went to check the alternator warning light with a local engineer. He identified the problem quite quickly; the starter that Neils had replaced had inadvertently trapped a cable going to the battery, causing intermittent charging.

An aerial view of Reykjavik (file photo).

Without electricity the engine would carry on running but we would lose all our radio contact and navigation systems. It could be repaired but the starter yet again needed to be removed. The engineer happened to have a spare gear pinion for the faulty starter and it seemed a good idea for both jobs to be done at the same time. Two days were needed as the workshop was quite busy.

With more time to spare Denis and I decided to explore Iceland for a couple of days. Iceland is certainly an appropriate name for a country with a lot of ice, but, in the summer, the capital Reykjavik has no ice or snow and is warm in the sun. However it is the only country where I have walked out of a restaurant not because of the food, but the prices! Iceland has to import a lot of its food and costs are therefore comparatively high. We had already spent a fortune in Greenland and were dismayed to find Iceland virtually equally expensive.

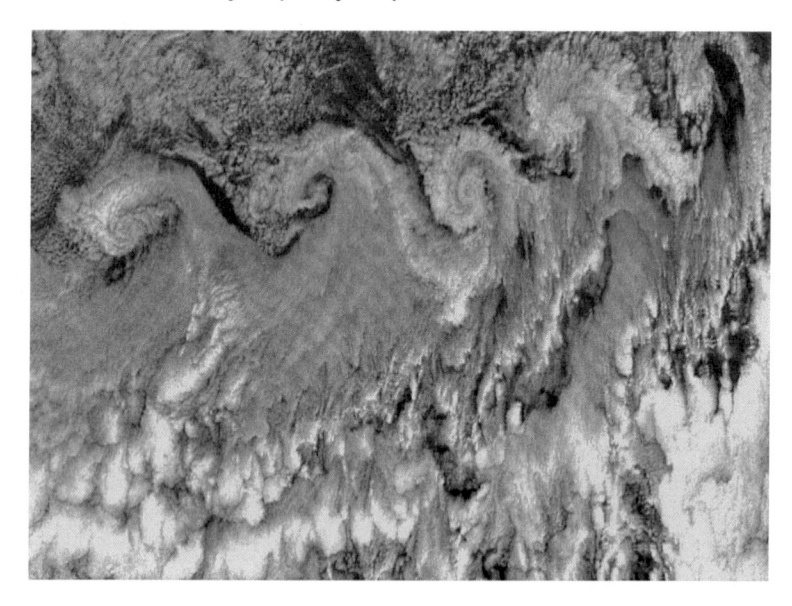

This rather unusual image photographed from a satellite shows a unique weather system between Iceland and Norway. It is hard to believe that what you are looking at is cloud - not unlike a group of Catherine Wheels at some monster Guy Fawkes party. The resultant weather is severe wind shear with speeds in excess of 200 miles per hour. You can imagine (or probably do not want to) the turbulence created in this aerial maelstrom, something for which pilots are ever vigilant – especially crossing the North Atlantic! (File photo).

Whilst waiting for the Warrior to be made ready we wandered around the city and included a visit to the historic Cathedral of Reykjavik. The older part of the city and port were bustling with activity, and the fish market had an amazing variety of marine life, much of which we had not seen before. No doubt some of it went to our hotel, as the evening meal of fish was `out of this world` and absolutely delicious.

The Warrior was ready on schedule but unfortunately the weather was not! Head winds were forecasted for the next few days, and we just did not have enough fuel capacity to risk the journey to Scotland. We made the decision that with so many delays we ought to go back by schedule airline and do some of Denis's urgent aerial photography work. The return to Iceland could be made when conditions were more favourable

A Hop Towards The Haggis

Seated in the comfort of an Icelandic Air Boeing 737 we relaxed and planned the photographic jobs that needed doing back home. We were thinking about the poor unfortunate ferry pilot who had drawn the short straw and had to get the Cessna 336 back to England. Brian was about to embark on the journey, and if we had any more delays with the Piper Warrior, he was likely to get to the UK before us! In any event that didn't happen as `the old dog` broke down twice en route; much to Brian's consternation and to Denis's blood pressure as he needed the plane urgently for the ever increasing work load.

After a few days back in England dealing with the most urgent of our business problems we were heading back to Reykjavik. The repairs to the Warrior had been completed, and most importantly the weather had improved with the head wind dropping down to an acceptable level.

After our renewed association with large airports and their flying schedules, it was a relief to find ourselves once again in Reykjavik. Clearing Customs we headed straight to the engineers workshop to collect the Warrior. They had fixed both the starter and the alternator and not only did it start but the battery also charged.

I had filed a flight plan to Stornoway, Isle of Lewis, in the Outer Hebrides, as Glasgow my main destination being a little further was on the limit of our fuel endurance. I put Faeroe Islands as a further alternative in case of problems. The Faeroes were not quite on our way but it seemed a good chance to maybe visit these islands, which I understand are quite unique. They are situated past the half way mark to the UK, as well as being halfway to Scandinavia or the outer islands of the Hebrides.

Air Traffic gave us our departure clearance and an initial heading towards the south routing us well clear of Keflavik International Airport. Although we had no head wind the weather was not much fun, gloomy and a little bouncy, and I could not climb very high as even at 10,000 feet we were in cloud. Going any higher would have meant getting iced up compromising the integrity of the plane. Freezing levels can be quite low in this area even in the summer, and this was something we were not cleared to fly into as the Warrior had no de-icing system.

It was dismal and tiring flying on instruments, but Denis came to the rescue with Icelandic sandwiches and drink which he had purchased from a little café in Reykjavík near the workshop hangar.

236

At one point we lost radio communication with Air Traffic Control, but fortunately Icelandic Air in an Airbus 320 was above us and we could report our position to them calling on the international open channel 121.50. We could not see where we were going and there was poor radar coverage in the area. However in this neighborhood there were so few small planes around that the chances of flying into one were not too considerable. To rephrase that, I doubt if there were any! Air Traffic advised us that NATO had some war games going on in the area off Scotland and we were asked to give the ships a wide berth, as military aircraft were also in the vicinity.

With a light tailwind our progress was slow; the weather at Faeroes Islands was relayed to us by a Norwegian Airline - it is truly international in the air! Sadly, the forecast was low cloud and poor visibility and as the approach is quite demanding, I decided to carry on to Stornoway to land and refuel before continuing to the UK mainland. This meant going close to the NATO war games but with little choice we carried on through the gloom.

Meanwhile Stornoway were attempting by relay radio to contact the man in charge of the NATO ships to make them aware of our location. Fortunately for all concerned, they succeeded, though we did get a ticking off from the war games controller for infringing on their activities and messing up their playtime. However, the choice was heading for the Hebrides or asking them if we could land on the aircraft carrier, *(which was bound to be included in the fleet)* in order that we could refuel – now that would have raised some eyebrows! However, they weren't too thrilled that we were in their vicinity and sent up a Harrier to check on us. The pilot did not get too close and he did wave a friendly greeting *(we hope)*. Afterwards the Air Traffic Controller told us that he hoped that we did not mind but the Harrier was using us for target practice! Apparently only with an infra-red gun site, and the pilot had been told not to start shooting as it would create a lot paper work! Denis and I would have not been too pleased either.

Receiving clearance to land at Stornoway Airport after our long flight from Reykjavik, the Scottish Islands appeared out of the gloom looking quite intimidating. Granite rocks protruded through the odd cloud giving a `Jurassic Park` impression. Descending to 1,000 feet above the rolling green seas of the north Atlantic crashing onto the rocks, did nothing to alleviate the feeling. After landing, civilization appeared at the end of the runway, and I seem to recall that Prince Charles tried to land an RAF transport plane on this runway with disastrous results. He overran the runway and did quite a bit of damage, but fortunately there were no injuries to personnel. It does not matter who you are, without constant practice these accidents will happen.

Switching off the Warrior's engine, Denis and I were both relieved to have got the Warrior to Great Britain so we celebrated with a hot cup of coffee in the canteen whilst the plane received a full tank of fuel. Friendly people as Islanders invariably are, they obtained the latest weather from Glasgow for our onward flight, and with the formalities completed we set off for the mainland. Flying over the northwest Scottish coast and towards the City airport reminded me how beautiful and desolate parts of our own country can be, with rugged mountains, deep valleys and little sign of life. People talk about the south island of New Zealand and how incredible the country is with its mountains and valleys. In flying around Great Britain doing aerial survey work, I know that our country also has all the beauty and ruggedness of other lands.

Flying in and out of cloud it was reassuring when contacting Glasgow Approach to hear a cheerful greeting. You can feel quite isolated in a small plane even if you have a companion with you. There is nowhere to move, even stretching your legs is difficult and after several hours you just want out! The radar vectors from Air Traffic guided me in and out of the rain showers down to the runway, whereupon the plane's wheels touched the tarmac welcoming us back to our side of the `*pond*`. After clearing Customs we headed off to the local airport hotel for a well-deserved rest, and haggis for supper. We were nearing the end of a special trip.

South Across The Border

Bright and early the following morning, with all the rain cleared away there was an excellent summer's day ahead. With full tanks, and thinking of home, we set off from Glasgow Airport heading due south to Fairoaks.

Flying over Gretna Green on the border, we were soon overhead Carlisle Airport, which reminded me that in a couple of months time I had to fly my brother-in-law from Germany to Gretna Green for a `classic wedding`. He and his bride wanted the marriage ceremony to have an unusual setting, and thought that this well documented and famous location would be that place! On the old coaching route between London and Edinburgh, Gretna Green was the first village reached once you entered Scotland. After Lord Hardwick's marriage act in 1754 outlawed marriage in England without paternal consent before the age of 21, young couples started to elope *'over the border'* to Gretna Green, where they could be married at 16 years of age. The residents of the small village of Gretna were well known for helping run-away couples, and many an inn and watering station along the route could be counted on to *'accidentally'* delay any pursuers, thus allowing the couples to safely reach Gretna. When I actually did the wedding trip, Carlisle Airport was virtually closed due to inclement weather, and with no real navigation aids at the Airport, I managed to get in at the third attempt. That was lucky and enabled the marriage to go ahead at Gretna Green. Otherwise, it might have been a disappointing wedding further north in Glasgow!

Clearing Scottish Control, we continued down the *airways* passing over Manchester and Birmingham and received clearance to head to London and home. It is quite amazing how built up and congested are the Midlands. With motorways crossing cities, towns and rural areas, it is no wonder people get lost. That is an advantage of flying – it's easier to go in a straight line *(well most of the time)*. The flight was a peaceful end to the long journey. With pleasant weather and no delays, as we got further south we were cleared to descend below the busy Heathrow Control sector. We dropped out of the airways at Henley-on-Thames and away from the *big guys*. Fairoaks welcomed us back in their usual friendly way, and after some 4,800 miles, with many different airports and adventures, Denis and I were home at last. The coffee in the airport's little café tasted the same as it always did – unpalatable – but drinking it there was a certain satisfaction in realising that we were well and truly back.

A few days later, I flew the Warrior from Fairoaks over the South Downs to Shoreham-on-Sea. The plane too, had experienced some weeks of adventure, and our last little flight together over the green hills was certainly a gentle ending to a great journey. I turned in a graceful arc towards Shoreham airport, and received clearance to land. My client was excitedly waving as I taxied to the apron.

Another delivery and importation into the UK and change of registration into a British identity. Yet one more American plane in the UK – what a pity that the British government in the late 40`s decided that there was no future in light aircraft. In fact, the British failed miserably in the development of airliners in general. The American aircraft industry succeeded in dominating the world for many years; sadly, Britain never caught up.

The End Of A Hop

The Piper Seneca, larger and better equipped than the Warrior. It was off to Lisbon, Portugal, via Santiago de Compostela, northwest Spain, and another story; but no European flying can ever replace a flight via the Northern Route of the world!

243

INFORMATION

The path to obtain a professional licence is in fact quite a sacrifice of time and money. Most would-be pilots have to self-fund the training with no guarantee of work at the end of the hard struggle. Many have put up their homes for security and borrowed vast sums of money to achieve their desired career. Apart from the monetary side of things, one has to be in perfect medical health and fitness in order to pass the stringent medical checks.

Being a pilot is a little like being a *jack-of-all-trades*. The following attributes are desirable: good at geography and navigation, an aptitude for electrical and mechanical engineering, the ability to lead as well as to work in a team, an intimate knowledge of weather systems, have rapid positive reactions to an emergency, be disciplined and reliable, and last but not least - not afraid of heights! After all that, and providing all the exams are passed, the starting salary is so low it is an embarrassment to mention a figure. However it improves; when you become captain of a large airliner then you are `top dog` and the earnings are well worth the effort.

A lot of would-be airline pilots normally need between 750 – 1,000 hours before an airline will look at them, so they become flying instructors on small planes to build up their hours. Some even fly small `business` planes doing charter and aerial work etc. to increase their experience, and to log valuable hours.

For those not too familiar with flying terms, below is a brief summary. *(It is not possible to be comprehensive on this subject without taking my book off in another direction, so this is purely a guideline.)*

PPL (*private pilot's licence*) is a basic pilot's licence for those that wish only to fly outside the main Controlled airspace in good weather and in sight of the ground.

IMC *(instrument metrological conditions)* is an additional rating on the PPL for those wishing to venture further airfield, armed with some basic navigation training and some practice in flying into cloud.

CPL (*commercial pilot's licence*) is a professional licence but without an IR *(instrument rating)* it is not much use. Most commercial pilots would study for the IR rating at the same time as the CPL. It is effectively a study in navigational aids, aviation law, metrology etc. The CPL/IR pilot is able to engage as captain in commercial charter, and aerial survey flying. He can also fly the airways of the world as co-pilot in training with the main airlines.

The final hurdle comes when obtaining the ATPL (*Air Transport Pilots Licence*). It is more a written exam and type rating qualification rather than actual flying, and is the licence required for piloting airliners around the world.

You will also need to have obtained a radio operators licence, a VHF (*Very High Frequency)* certificate for normal flying, and a HF *(High Frequency)* licence for ocean crossing.

A medical licence is necessary, and indeed you will need to obtain one early in your career, ensuring that you are fit enough to fly safely into the wild blue yonder.

During training and after qualifying, the pilot has to be type rated; another set of tests to complete and pass before being let loose on the aviation world. A pilot would start with a humble Cessna 150 and move up in stages to the massive Boeing 747 – 600 and the Airbus A380. As each plane becomes more complex – so does the rating, thus ensuring that you are `up to speed` on the planes you fly. Various books covering all aspects of the licence are available from a choice of aviation outlets.

I personally spent some £20,000 in the 1980's *(it would be a lot more today)* to obtain my unrestricted commercial licence complete with the instrument rating, HF and VHF radio licences. Unfortunately, when I qualified and started my preparations to join the airlines fate struck a blow. At the end of the 1980's, America went into a deep recession and two giant airlines went broke: Pan American and Eastern Airways ceased flying *(both closed the hangar doors to the world in 1991)*. I could not compete with the large number of highly qualified and experienced pilots who were then sadly out of work. As a result I stopped my rating one-step above the Piper Seneca stage, and had many great years of part-time flying clocking up nearly 4,000 hours. It wasn't with the Airlines, but I did attain my dream, if only in flying small planes.

References

I have read far too many aviation books over the years so it would be impossible to list them all. Sufficient to say, I had learnt a great deal from many present day authors, as well as those who were writing in the early part of the 20th century, detailing the emergence and progress of aviation.

The Oxford Dictionary of Weather
By Storm Dunlop, Fellow of the Royal Astronomical & Metrology Society.

True North   George Erikson

The Cloud Spotters Guide   By Gavin Pretor-Pinney

Fate is the Hunter   Ernest K Gann

Straight on Till Morning   Biography of Beryl Markham

Jane's Aircraft – reference book

Ins & outs of Ferry Flying   Don & Julia Lee Brownie

Alone in the sky   Jean Batten

West with night   Beryl Markham

GEO Group for Earth Observation (satellite weather imagery)

The Balloon Factory   Alexander Frater

All books worth reading

There are numerous other books available by various authors writing about Amy Johnson, the Wright Brothers, Charles Lindbergh, and Amelia Earhart.